Playing with Trains

Entrepreneur Bill Galpin weds a sharp eye for spotting talent in others with a desire to realise their inventions against the stultifying apathy of the Establishment. But as his egotistical flair for self-publicity intensifies, his personal relationship with his daughter and son deteriorates.

Stephen Poliakoff, born in 1952, was appointed Writer in Residence at the National Theatre for 1976 and the same year won the Evening Standard's Most Promising Playwright award for *Hitting Town* and *City Sugar*. He also won a BAFTA Award for the Best Single Play of 1980 for *Caught on a Train*. His plays and films include *Clever Soldiers* (1974), *The Carnation Gang* (1974), *Hitting Town* (1975), *City Sugar* (1975), *Heroes* (1975), *Strawberry Fields* (1977), *Stronger than the Sun* (1977), *Shout Across the River* (1978), *American Days* (1979), *The Summer Party* (1980), *Bloody Kids* (1980), *Caught on a Train* (1980), *Favourite Nights* (1981), *Soft Targets* (1982), *Runners* (1983), *Breaking the Silence* (1984), *Coming in to Land* (1987), *Hidden City* (1988) and *She's Been Away* (1989).

by the same author

AMERICAN DAYS
BREAKING THE SILENCE
COMING IN TO LAND
FAVOURITE NIGHTS & CAUGHT ON A TRAIN
HITTING TOWN & CITY SUGAR
RUNNERS & SOFT TARGETS
SHE'S BEEN AWAY & HIDDEN CITY
SHOUT ACROSS THE RIVER
STRAWBERRY FIELDS
THE SUMMER PARTY

POLIAKOFF PLAYS: ONE
(Clever Soldiers, Hitting Town, City Sugar,
Shout Across the River, American Days, Strawberry Fields)

STEPHEN POLIAKOFF

Playing with Trains

Methuen Drama

ACT ONE

Scene One

ROXANNA *standing in a spot, front stage left. She is dressed in school uniform. At the beginning of the action she is 18 years old. She is pulling hard at her school tie, loosening it round her neck. She has a light Midlands accent.*

ROXANNA. July 15th – could be a very important date, a date in my progress, I suppose, in our fortunes.

It's bloody hot, anyway, and I still have to wear this for a few more days, for the last time. I have started a countdown till the end of term, hour by hour.

But the great news today *is*, or possibly very grim news – depends how you look at it. And I'm not at all sure how I'm looking at it, because today is the day when I realised we are about to be hit – by money. A great deal of money. It could come pouring through the door at any moment. Or it could not.

It depends on him of course.

Lights up behind ROXANNA, and she turns. The set is comprised of russet-coloured walls, which remain throughout the action.

Across the stage is a great pile of packing, half a lifetime of belongings, old suitcases, large boxes crammed tight, old armchairs, some of which have split, tables on top of each other, carpets rolled up, some rugs unrolled, cricket bats, pictures, chairs with their legs sticking in the air, some sixties lamps and several gramophones are prominent. Clothes too, lots of shoes and boots, children's toys and books.

Most of this is closely piled together in a large heap, packed tight enough for someone to walk on. But there are smaller outcrops, spread around, including smaller battered suitcases.

Hot summer light.

ROXANNA *picks something off the floor, an old toy, and throws it on the pile as* DANNY *enters. He is two years younger than* ROXANNA, *in grey trousers, pale shirt, carrying a bicycle with a twisted, mangled, front wheel. He has an enthusiastic, open manner, and the same light Midlands accent, difficult to place exactly.*

DANNY (*with mangled bicycle*). What about this? At last I've found something we don't have to take. We can leave this behind surely?

ROXANNA. No, we can't. We're taking everything. You never know when we may need that.

DANNY. Really? What on earth are you expecting to happen!

ROXANNA (*smiles*). And I may just be able to fix it.

DANNY. OK here – (ROXANNA *takes bicycle*, DANNY *staring towards pile*.) who would have thought all this junk could have come out of our house?

ROXANNA, *having glanced at it, tosses bicycle onto pile. She moves confidently. Despite her age, she has great natural authority.*

ROXANNA. We have no idea how long this is going to last, Danny, anyway.

DANNY. If it begins at all that is.

ROXANNA. What do you mean?

DANNY. He just turned down the deal.

ROXANNA. I don't believe it, again! – he can't do that.

DANNY. He can. He's asking for more.

ROXANNA (*startled*). For more! We're moving house, he's bought another house already, he has to say yes.

DANNY. He's asking for so much now! Because each time he says no, they want him more, to buy him out even more, there's no limit it seems to what he can ask for.

ROXANNA. Of course there is. He's in danger of over-doing it. (*Sharp.*) And he's got to get a guarantee on jobs as well.

DANNY. I think it's brilliant. (*Moving suitcases.*) If we could find the phone that's buried somewhere under all this, maybe we could listen in.

ROXANNA. Go on! (*Anarchic smile.*) Find the phone, I want to interrupt negotiations, tell him to take it.

FRANCES *enters, in her early twenties, working-class girl, intelligent eyes, unafraid. She's carrying two bulky portable gramophones, piled on each other.*

ROXANNA. And who's that?

FRANCES. Your father's new assistant, Frances.

DANNY (*giving a welcoming smile*). So he's got an extra secretary now too.

FRANCES. Acquired a new assistant, that's right. (DANNY *offering to take gramophones.*) I can manage.

ROXANNA (*glancing towards where the phone might be*). This better bloody work, hadn't it! (*Moving forward, warm smile.*) Hello, we can't shake hands, obviously. What are you doing with those?

FRANCES. I just arrived for my interview. (*She heaves gramophones onto pile.*) After twenty seconds he said, 'You've got the job'.

ROXANNA. He took as long as that, did he?

FRANCES. Then he said, 'Take these, they're packing everything up in there'.

ROXANNA. Yes – he's right. We have to take the gramophones.

DANNY (*lifting lids of gramophones*). That's what all this is about.

FRANCES. About these gramophones here?

DANNY. Yes, the automatic turntable, his firm created it when they were a very small concern, they developed the idea, he found the money somehow and it totally altered the manufacture of the gramophone.

ROXANNA (*very authoritative*). The automatic record changer existed before of course Danny, but they totally revolutionised the design . . .

DANNY. And so now they're miles ahead of the field because . . . Roxanna's much better at all that than me – at technical things.

ROXANNA. The design change enabled it to be made much cheaper, mass produced much more easily. I'll do a drawing later, show you what they did. So he makes gramophones, lots and lots of them.

DANNY. And, all being well, he's about to be bought out – for a very large sum.

FRANCES. I joined at the right time it seems.

ROXANNA (*excited smile*). Maybe. And if he does the right thing (*Warm.*) otherwise this will be the shortest job you've ever had. (*Moving.*) Jesus, the smell from this pile.

DANNY (*embarrassed*). Roxy . . . I can't smell anything.

ROXANNA *climbing onto part of pile, walking along the top of it, looking down at them.*

ROXANNA (*to* FRANCES). *You* can smell it, can't you?

FRANCES (*smiles*). Oh yes, very clearly.

ROXANNA (*on heap, moving along plateau at top*). Starting at this end, the deep aroma of really bad times, when money was always disappearing, the smell of those foul chairs, ingrained with all those meals of baked beans and burnt toast.

DANNY. Yes, when we had to sell the car . . . when things got pretty bad.

ROXANNA (*moving further along pile, standing on the objects*). And then things temporarily looked better, moving upmarket here, around these formica tables, nice cluster of anglepoise lamps here, and then a bad wobble . . . (*Kicking an object with her foot.*) followed by a plunge down, into dark times, round these stained carpets and overgloves with holes, when Mum left (*To* FRANCES.) when she'd had *enough* and cleared out.

DANNY. Cleared out so effectively, we never see her, she's in the US and gone. (*He smiles.*) We didn't even get an invitation to the re-marriage.

ROXANNA (*lightly, reaching another section of piles*). And then here, when he was so busy there were no new saucepans, no new clothes for us, everything has its handle missing, and you have to wade through the hundreds of letters he sent to the local press here, an obscure electrical engineer bombarding them with ideas about every possible products – from the suburbs of Nottingham!

Shower of papers falls to ground.

And then here, he produces something people seem to want, and so we hit the new coffee table, and the oriental rugs, and his collection of unread 'Book of the Month' and here I am at last standing on good times, if he doesn't fuck everything up now.

BILL *enters*. ROXANNA *is still on top of the pile of books and belongings and is staring down at him.*

BILL *is casually dressed, a sense of contained energy about him. He's in his early forties, with a startling informal quality in his manner, in the way he addresses his children. His voice can be surprisingly quiet but then change almost in mid-sentence, becoming extremely animated. He has a light Nottinghamshire accent.*

ROXANNA (*staring down at BILL*). Did you hear that?

BILL. Yes.

ROXANNA. So have you?

DANNY. What's happening Dad?

BILL. Why's everybody in such a hurry? Now – don't either of you shout, but I've turned them down.

ROXANNA. Down! You've turned them down. Again . . . !

DANNY. I knew you'd take them all the way, as far as you can.

ROXANNA. If you wait too long they won't need to buy you out, they'll have developed a new kind of gramophone themselves.

BILL (*looks up at her*). Oh I should have you consulted you, should I?

ROXANNA. Of course. (*To* FRANCES.) Though he hates to admit it – he sometimes does.

BILL. Come down from there, come on. (*Lifting* ROXANNA *down, holding onto her.*) I bet my children have been as rude as usual and haven't introduced themselves – have you?

FRANCES. Half introductions – they started and never finished.

BILL. This is my daughter, Roxanna – her mother gave her that strange name, I didn't – and Roxanna is the trouble round here (*He smiles.*) though she has her uses, which include constantly provoking me. You will notice she even has to wear her school uniform in a perverse way – little anarchic flourish.

Looks across.

And that's Danny . . .

DANNY (*nervous smile*). Yes. This is me.

Slight pause.

BILL. And Danny is quite sensible – usually.

ROXANNA (*tone warm, combative, totally as an equal*). Have you seen, Dad, on the pile here – all sorts of things we were forbidden as kids have bobbed up to the surface, for all to see.

BILL (*lightly*). What do you mean – you weren't forbidden anything as kids!

ROXANNA. You didn't know about them though, did you?

DANNY. Like Roxanna's comics and shocking red tights, and packets of fags, and her weird diaries with yellow covers.

ROXANNA (*indicates pile*). Not to mention Danny's schoolboy porn splashing everywhere.

BILL (*grins*). What makes you think I didn't know about them anyway?

ROXANNA (*straight back*). Because I hid them too well. And if you had known – you would undoubtedly have stolen some of the fags. But you will also notice how my beautiful technical drawings and diagrams are on display. Pride of place, in fact.

BILL. Yes, not bad.

ROXANNA (*mocking*). High praise! (*Right up to him.*) Dad if you blow this deal now . . .

BILL (*straight back*). *If* I blow it – what. (*Combative smile.*) Little girl.

ROXANNA *moves*.

You're not usually this cautious.

ROXANNA (*swings round*). I'm not unpacking all this for a start! Do you realise how long this took – this is staying just as it is.

BILL. Yes, I see you've mashed this so tight together. (*Trying to pull chair free of the pile.*) squeezed it so close, it's not going to be easy to take down. (*Looks at her.*) Trying to make sure there's no turning back, are you?

ROXANNA. Of course there's no turning back now.

BILL (*slight grin*). Isn't there!

ROXANNA (*loudly but lightly*). I thought we were really getting out of this place at last. Out of this bloody town. You've bought a new house, you haven't sold this one, you need the money.

BILL. A small detail – the deal has to be good enough. (*To ROXANNA as if in reply.*) And have a guarantee about jobs! But it has to be a really improbable amount, otherwise it isn't worth taking, because I won't be able to do what I have in mind. (*To FRANCES, suddenly.*) What do you think?

FRANCES (*looking straight at him*). I agree.

BILL. You should say what you mean around here you know.

FRANCES. I gathered that. I haven't the slightest idea what you have in mind, but I like the sound of it. I agree with you.

BILL (*smiles*). You see, I have support here . . .

DANNY (*to ROXANNA*). You know how much he'll be worth – if he brings this off. I'm guessing, but it will be in seven figures.

BILL (*sharp*). Danny, stop it, that fact on its own is absolutely of no interest.

ROXANNA (*to BILL*). So why are you trying to push the price up so far then Dad?

BILL. You'll see.

ROXANNA (*sharp*). Who needs a lot of money! And (*Lightly.*) I'm not sure all this money will be good for you anyway. You'll probably go to seed, become flabby and destructive and boring, (*Provocative.*) go into steep decline.

BILL. You don't trust me. (*To* FRANCES.) They don't trust me.

DANNY. Of course we do.

ROXANNA (*straight at him, sharp smile*). Do we? Apart from everything else, I just don't want to have to put up with your cooking any more – every third day when it's your turn.

Phone rings, faint ring from under belongings.

BILL. If we can find the phone – which you've managed to bury – maybe we can do a deal.

ROXANNA (*urgent*). Don't play around any more Dad. Go and do it. (*As* BILL *unhurriedly moves debris to look for phone*.) Quick – take it on the other phone – go on!

Blackout.

Scene Two

ROXANNA *front stage, taking her school blazer off, and putting on a brightly coloured well-fitting sweater. Then she brushes her hair back, sharp, more mature, the schoolgirl image falling off with each stroke.*

ROXANNA (*tone excited, but wary*). May 17th. Guess what. (*The sweater going on.*) Unbelievable isn't it, but true. We are moving *again*. Yes. Another violent disruption because of a second new discovery. I've hardly had time to visit all the rooms in this house – in fact I've still to find at least two of the bathrooms. And all this because of a development in the the single reflex lens, pioneered in Japan in 1905.

As she speaks the second large pile comes onto the set. She watches it being added to the heap of belongings of the first scene. This time it consists of luxurious junk, late sixties junk, two trolleys of it piled high, packed ready to move. There is a half unrolled snow white carpet too.

1905. Yes! A dramatic advance in camera design so far ahead of its time that nobody had done anything about it, even in Japan. And Dad, with a reasonably brilliant stroke, spotted this small English firm trying to redevelop the idea and going bust in the process and he poured and poured money at them, helped them modify it, and then desperately looked around for a British company to come in with him to mass produce the cameras. But there have been no takers naturally. (*She smiles.*) They ran in the opposite direction as soon as they saw him coming.

So he's had to join up with the . . . Japanese. Yes, having seized an idea they themselves had missed, (*Lightly.*) it looks like making Dad another fortune of course and this time quite a big one . . . the gramophone tycoon has struck again. (*Slight pause.*) He seems to have backed the right idea.

Lights up on set. BILL packing, caged energy. He has taken his jacket off, in same shirt and trousers, but striking, new, fashionable shoes.

ROXANNA. So this is what you had in mind, was it?

> BILL *moving by the pile.*

BILL. What do you mean?

ROXANNA. What you're going to do with yourself from now on, moving house every year, throwing them away like paper cups, had this one, so . . . (*Makes a chucking movement over her shoulder.*)

BILL. This has been a disaster hasn't it – this mansion, being behind an electric fence, a total disaster!

ROXANNA. It might have helped if we had ever unpacked.

BILL. It doesn't suit us living like this.

ROXANNA. I am not sure it suits anybody (*Pulling at a chair tightly packed in pile.*) – chairs tend to be quite useful you know.

BILL. No – in this style (*Energised.*) I have the swimming pool here totally retiled –

ROXANNA. To impress the young girls you have lazing around here.

BILL. – and it is immediately over-run with frogs. They even seem to have a special species here, the Chertsey frog, hops around from the pools of the surrounding pop stars.

ROXANNA. Slightly stoned and over-weight.

BILL. I give a couple of enormous garden parties, like you are meant to, and it pours with rain, a deluge for each one! And all the time we are here the burglar alarm is ringing – going off in the middle of the night, police cars roaring down the drive.

ROXANNA. Yes, my only memories of this house will be endless white rooms and burglar alarms going off. (*Slight smile.*) We've been strangers in somebody else's place.

BILL. I have never understood how people can shut themselves away in large houses, cage themselves up, ridiculous way to live, who needs it . . .

ROXANNA. Now he realises!

BILL (*sharp smile*). My puritan daughter – I had to see for myself . . . didn't I?

ROXANNA (*straight back*). Did you? (*Touching him.*) Don't do it again.

BILL. No.

ROXANNA. Still trying to get into a gentlemen's club are you?

BILL. Oh yes, very definitely.

ROXANNA (*warm*). Haven't they all turned you down yet!

BILL. No, no, I'm waiting to hear back from the Saville Club any day.

ROXANNA (*warm*). I'm going to have to do something about your taste you know.

BILL (*smiling at her*). You reckon so.

FRANCES *entering with some garish ornamental belongings.*

ROXANNA (*staring at these*). Definitely! (*Warm.*) And did I actually see you with a *book* last week? With a hardcover even! Reading some literature for once.

BILL (*back at her*). It's possible . . .

FRANCES (*confident, excited*). The trucks are coming soon, I hope you haven't left anything, should be doing your last round of checking. I'm taking no blame for what's left behind, I warn you!

BILL (*smiles at FRANCES, moves among luggage*). She gets ruder by the day . . .

MICK *enters, carrying more belongings, a gangling boy of about 22.*

ROXANNA. Who's that?

BILL. Oh that's Mick.

MICK *grunts.*

BILL. I'm backing some of his ideas. Interesting engineering modifications, some fine drawings, one or two possibly remarkable inventions.

ROXANNA. Oh really! So why's he having to help us move house?

BILL. He offered to.

MICK (*surly*). He asked me to.

ROXANNA. An offer you couldn't refuse. Obviously. (*Turning to BILL.*) Having inventors to do your packing now, are we! (*Lightly to MICK.*) I should get away from here as soon as possible, that's my advice, run like mad. Get away from him!

MICK. Why?

ROXANNA (*lightly*). Because he's probably only playing at this, acquiring some new distractions.

FRANCES (*indicating MICK*). I don't know what his inventions are like, but he's a bloody good removal man. Can lift anything. (*To MICK.*) Come on, one last search of the house.

MICK *and FRANCES exit.*

BILL (*indicating* MICK *as he goes*). No, this is serious Roxanna. You will see.

ROXANNA. Will I? When?

DANNY *running on with more, new garish belongings.*

DANNY. These nearly got left behind.

ROXANNA (*quiet, eyeing these belongings*). We don't have to take everything do we . . .

DANNY. I love moving. (*With paper to* BILL.) You know what else I found, the map of millionaires I made. My research, millionaires in five European countries where their homes are – I've marked the spot – how much they're worth, and where you come in the list, in the league table I've made of the wealthy.

BILL. Not now Danny, not now, OK.

ROXANNA. I don't think he's in the mood for that somehow.

DANNY. You are moving up the table fast, although there's a long way to go of course. I'll show it to you later.

BILL *is pulling chair out of tightly packed pile, having to yank it with real force.*

BILL. I want to talk to you both. (*Moving with chair.*) It has not pleased me, the business about the camera – having to lose the idea back to Japan.

ROXANNA. You tried all you could.

BILL (*clicking his fingers*). Something else has just gone too you know, which nobody here seems to have noticed at all – a breakthrough with magnetic tape, audio and video recording.

ROXANNA (*immediately*). Being able to squeeze tracks tightly together on the same tape? Be able to really shrink in size, won't they?

BILL (*sharp*). That's right, Roxanna. It'll probably be extraordinarily successful. (*Suddenly powerful.*) But it's not going to keep on happening – not if I can help it. (*Loud.*) Something has to be done . . . (*Glance at* ROXANNA.) You know Roxanna your Cambridge entrance result, the more I think about it, the better it seems.

ROXANNA (*lightly*). Yes, you crammed me well didn't you?

BILL (*anarchic smile, stabbing finger*). It was nearly what I expected.

ROXANNA (*warm*). Good – then I can take a rest then, can't I!

BILL (*looks round*). And Danny . . .

DANNY *looks at him.*

. . . we're still seeing how things are turning out. (*Ruffling DANNY's hair.*) But they seem to be going quite well too . . .

DANNY. Yes, Dad . . .

BILL *looks at both of them.*

BILL. Roxanna's going to study engineering I hope. Danny it looks like being physics.

DANNY. Yes, I think so Dad.

BILL (*moving along belongings on pile*). Christ, there's a lot here now isn't there. (*He turns.*) Now you two, I just want to find this out. Do you want – money? (*Anarchic smile.*) I don't particularly want to give it to you, but do you want to be set up with an income? (*Looks at them.*) Some money now?

DANNY. No, no, totally not. We're going to do it ourselves.

ROXANNA. I wouldn't take a penny.

BILL. Come on there's no need to overdo it! Jesus . . . it sounds like you've been rehearsing between you. Say what you feel, not what you think I want to hear, I'm talking real money you understand, not pocket money, real money. (*Sharp.*) Say now . . . do you want it?

ROXANNA (*strong*). We don't want it Dad. Absolutely not.

BILL. Good. That's what I knew you'd say.

Blackout.

Scene Three

In the blackout, music bursting down, the theme tune of a television programme, a voice booms out, Ladies and Gentlemen, live from Shepherds Bush, 'In the Hot Seat' *(Theme tune rises and dips.)* and to face the probing questions of Vernon Boyce tonight is – dynamic entrepreneur and flamboyant businessman, the gramophone tycoon, Bill Galpin.

> *Swivel chair in the middle of the stage in spot, by itself. Everything else is in darkness. Vernon Boyce fires his questions outside the lighted ring, seated in silhouette.*

> BILL *walks on and sits on chair, alone in spotlight. He is wearing a new grey jacket, same trousers and shoes.*

BOYCE. Mr Galpin, welcome. What does money mean to you?

BILL *(his voice throughout a mixture of the quiet tentative, and then loud and direct)*. Money . . . ? Money itself, money means nothing to me of course. OK, nothing may be a bit simple . . . not much. It's what you do –

BOYCE *(cutting him off)*. Many people watching may not believe that.

BILL *(briskly)*. No, no it's true. I like having enough of course, I didn't always . . . have, but when you've made some money through luck or circumstance or whatever, it really doesn't take any special talent or intelligence to make more of it – it really doesn't, it's –

BOYCE. Are you a vain person?

BILL. So you're going to shoot straight from the hip right from the start.

BOYCE. They're all going to be straight from the hip questions, you've obviously not watched the programme.

BILL. Oh yes *(He smiles.)* I've watched your show, it's attempting to be a popular, cruder version – isn't it – of an earlier more famous show, when the interviewer also lurked . . . in the darkness.

BOYCE. Thank you, I'm reassured to hear you're a regular viewer. To return to the question – would you be surprised if people called you a vain person?

BILL (*moving in chair*). I've never thought about it, till this moment, maybe not. (*Sharp smile.*) I'm no saint certainly . . . I think I am capable of certain things, yes, which given a chance I want to talk ab-

BOYCE. Please don't move the chair, the hot seat.

The chair has slid back slightly, out of the spotlight.

If you do move it like that, you just disappear, vanish suddenly into total darkness.

BILL *moving chair back. Edge of spotlight, half lit, during the following exchange he moves again, into full central brightness.*

BILL. Disappear? Into blackness. I'll try to keep still then. (*He smiles.*) Depends on the questions.

BOYCE. So how *would* you describe yourself – as a tycoon? A flamboyant tycoon who . . .

BILL. I keep on hearing that expression, no. As a businessman, entrepreneur, and I hope, unfashionable as this is, a patron. I am not an inventor myself, though I can make suggestions sometimes about ideas, modifications, but I want to discover and back –

BOYCE (*cutting him off*). But you live a very flamboyant lifestyle don't you, in large houses, being photographed with pop stars, holding great parties that –

BILL. My parties tend not to be successes. Disasters in fact.

BOYCE. But since you've burst on the business scene, you've had a fabulously successful few years.

BILL. Fabulous no, good yes.

BOYCE (*loud*). Is it important to you how much you are worth?

BILL. You want me to tell you in public, how much I am worth?

BOYCE. I want to know how important to you that is.

BILL. Money . . . money again. You don't want to accept what I tell you do you – you want to go on asking these voyeuristic questions about how –

BOYCE. You think they're voyeuristic? . . . Are you guilty about having made so much?

BILL. Certainly not.

BOYCE. But you are an extremely rich man?

BILL. A rich man.

BOYCE. An enormously rich man.

BILL. A rich man.

BOYCE. And you're an ambitious man too, after the years of obscurity, there is a feverish, almost anarchic energy, as if you are making up for lost time?

BILL. I want to try . . .

BOYCE. And in the way you've spoken out on several issues. You're a man in a hurry –

BILL. I'm not in such a hurry that I don't have time to finish the answer to your questions, something I'm finding extremely . . .

BOYCE. And you haven't exactly hidden from the attention you've received have you? Like coming on this show for instance –

BILL. No, because I intend – and I'm going to get this out whether you like it or not – I intend to back certain things that interest me, to sponsor bright young engineers and scientists. There is an extraordinary inventiveness in this country, and I wish to publicise that and ask are we encouraging it enough?

BOYCE. And make money out of it at the same time, obviously.

BILL (*smiles*). It's important not to go broke naturally.

BOYCE. So you're appealing to people to share your enthusiasms, you are a person of sudden enthusiasms are you not?

BILL. No, no, constant enthusiasms.

BOYCE. You were very quick to correct that, why is that so important to you?

BILL. I've always had intense enthusiasms since I was a boy. For better or worse I'm not inclined towards the arts, but to machines of all kinds, and also bridges, buildings, viaducts, and pipes.

BOYCE. Pipes! Are you serious?

BILL. Oh yes. Good drainage works are very exciting. (*Sharp smile.*) Don't you find? Among the most exciting things, can have a peculiar, unique kind of beauty. I trained as a civil engineer . . .

BOYCE. Despite the blaze of publicity which you've encouraged – why are you so private about your background, your family?

BILL. Am I? I don't think I am. My father ran an ironmonger store and before you jump in and ask (*Smiles.*) yes, it could be that is where my love affair with metal objects began! And my children . . .

BOYCE. Ah, yes, you have two children, don't you?

BILL. I'm quite proud of them, my son and daughter, Danny and Roxanna. My son's finishing his education, my daughter Roxanna is . . . (*Slight pause.*) a very talented engineer. More girls should do it of course – in fact she shows every sign of being, possibly, brilliant at engineering.

BOYCE. So there'll be two of you! Two of you to watch, will there?

BILL. You make it sound like a threat! (*Sharp smile.*) Maybe there will – she can be both more sensible and more fearless than me at times, (*Looks around.*) very possibly there will be two of us, yes . . .

BOYCE. Now, you would accept, Mr Galpin, that when you've made the amounts of money you have, that brings with it a considerable degree of power?

BILL (*moving in chair, both chair and him sliding out of spot*). Depends what sort of power you are talking about.

BOYCE. You've disappeared into utter darkness again Mr Galpin. (*Sharp.*) Literally removed yourself . . . Could you move the hot seat back, because you are totally invisible at the moment.

BILL *leans forward. Just his actual face visible, rest in darkness.*

BOYCE (*moving back into light, totally illuminated, incisive*). All I've said is – we're putting up buildings at the moment all around us, this extraordinary expansion of high rise buildings, which are based on a faulty engineering principle, calculated only to work in ideal conditions on totally flat ground. The whole basis of system building, which is what is being used because it's cheap, is that every part will fit absolutely perfectly into every other part, all right for an intricate machine like a watch but impossible in a building, which means the blocks going up now will begin to leak and crack, almost from birth!

BOYCE. This is getting very technical – please can we . . .

BILL. It's not technical – a child of three can understand it! It's important people don't glaze over when they hear such things, (*Moving in light.*) I can see you are glazing over. The viewers can't but I can tell you he's totally glazed all right.

BOYCE. I'm glazing over, because this is too specialised for a show like this. I want to return . . .

BILL (*cutting him off*). These buildings are unsound. It's going to be a massive billion pound failure over the next 20 years.

BOYCE. Mr Galpin this is not the Open University, no doubt you can arrange to appear on that as well, but we are here.

BILL (*cutting him off*). I don't know if there is going to be a record of this programme, whether the tape will be preserved, but I saw *now*, people will be dismantling some of these new buildings, blowing them up within a very few years.

BOYCE. I realise you are here to propagate your views Mr Galpin, but they are irrelevant to what concerns –

BILL. Irrelevant – how?

BOYCE. I don't want to come to blows about this, but we must resume the normal personal questions which is the point of . . .

BILL. I thought you wanted a fight! I was promised tough questions, but I had tougher questions than this in an interview I did for a school magazine last week.

BOYCE. You like using aggression do you?

BILL. Depends on whom. On you. Yes, at this precise moment, most certainly.

BOYCE. Let's take a look at these qualifications of yours shall we?

BILL. Why not. Absolutely! (*Ebullient.*) And let's take a look at you too – let's break down these artificial barriers, let's pull you into the light.

> BILL *slides his chair and then gets up in pursuit of* VERNON BOYCE.

BILL. So come on, let's see what's lurking here shall we.

BOYCE (*loud, urgent*). And that concludes tonight's show. Thank you and good night. Are we rolling? Music?

BILL. No, don't be bashful, let's shatter this gimmick shall we.

> *Pulling balding man into spot, both in spot for a second as music rolling.*

Let the viewers take a look at your 'qualifications'. That's right . . .

> *Blackout as music rolls.*

Scene Four

ROXANNA *leaning against the proscenium smoking, behind her sounds as if from a busy street, mixed with music as if from a busker. She's got heavy make-up on, her clothes late sixties, but not stereotyped, showing an unconventional taste.*

ROXANNA. October 13th – something odd happened today. Quite by chance, having not seen him for many weeks I met him in the street, in the middle of the West End, Dad – who by now hardly goes anywhere on foot.

It was like he'd willed the accidental meeting to happen, demanded that there I would be, right in his path, at that very moment.

He was wearing these startling clothes, in fact I saw his coat first, and then his strangely coloured shoes, of course, before I looked up and saw who was wearing them. As usual his efforts to be fashionable were just slightly off, slightly wrong, but the effect is typical of him, rather crude but also something more interesting, a sort of mixture of bludgeon and elegance.

And he was bearing down on me, bristling with energy, with the boy genius trotting at his heels.

BILL *enters dressed in a cashmere coat, unbuttoned, with its fine scarlet lining showing, and his gun-metal grey shoes. The effect is striking.* MICK *following him, in jeans and an anorak, and holding papers under his arm.*

ROXANNA. I thought I recognised that walk.

BILL. Roxanna – I might not have recognised you. (*Up close.*) What's all this? Smudges all over your face. (*Slight smile.*) You haven't been home for a while.

ROXANNA (*lightly*). If you go around looking like that – it's not surprising, how can I be seen with you?

BILL (*sharp smile*). What's wrong with the coat?

ROXANNA. I don't know what I'm going to do about your choice of clothes. (*Touches his collar.*) I was going to write any day now – I've been really busy.

BILL. Busy at what, what've you been up to?

ROXANNA. This and that. I'm hanging out with some interesting people. (*Lightly.*) You wouldn't like them. (*Tone changes.*) I thought you'd be angry with me still, after all those letters, after I quit the engineering course. Just for a year of course, quit university.

BILL. No. (*He smiles.*) Not worth the effort. OK – you need time to look around. I'll give it to you.

ROXANNA. Will you?

BILL. You want me to try to stop you – is that it? I'm not going to do that. (*Shrewd look.*) You'll come back when it's right.

ROXANNA. Yes, I know.

MICK (*very impatient*). We're going to be late you realise.

BILL. Yes – that means we must be. He never says anything usually, so obviously we're very late!

ROXANNA (*glancing at the boy, then back at* BILL). All these projects, I've lost count of them! And they're beginning to get written up in the papers as well –

BILL. You're reading about them then? Good.

ROXANNA (*close to him*). Can't help it, can I – you keep on sending me the cuttings. You should stop appearing on television so often you know, you're being over-exposed, but *if* you do any more, you have this extraordinary two-tone delivery you realise, you mumble and then right in the middle of the sentence you bark out the rest, there's no need for that.

BILL (*slight smile*). Any other lessons you want to give me?

MICK. Come on for chrissake – we mustn't be this late.

BILL. Yes – he's right. We're about to go and rip away some cobwebs, get his ideas away from some of the idiots who've been sitting on them. (*He smiles.*) A meeting I hope they're dreading. (*Moves, then suddenly turning back to her.*) Why don't you come and see? (*Quiet, inviting.*) Come on . . .

ROXANNA. I'd like to but – (*Slight pause.*) No, I can't Dad – not now. Another time . . .

Lights up on table and two chairs front stage left. GANT, *a slight blond man, in his early thirties, standing waiting.*

ROXANNA *watches them approach the table before she exits.* GANT *has a long pale expressive face, flapping hands, he is full of a sudden, surprising intensity.*

GANT. It's terrific, absolutely terrific, to see you here in person, to welcome you. Best thing that's happened to me all week.

BILL. That's the kind of greeting we were not expecting.

MICK. In the circumstances it's the least he can do.

BILL. Maybe we should come in again – see if it gets even better the second time.

GANT. I mean it.

BILL. Nevertheless this will be the only conversation we ever have (*Looks at him.*) unless we can work something out now.

GANT. Exactly. I feel the same.

BILL. This boy is gifted (*Dangerous smile.*) is he not? A little difficult, but genuinely very gifted. He looks at machines and structures with an original eye, sometimes startlingly original. *So where the hell are his designs?*

MICK (*loud*). What have you done with them?

BILL (*sharp, moving*). He comes out of nowhere – a tiny engineering firm in the Midlands, with spectacular ideas! You take options on his designs, an especially long option on one of the best, the quiet diesel engine.

MICK. Which has the potential for selling all over the world . . .

BILL. And you've been sitting on that idea for two-and-a-half years – doing absolutely nothing.

GANT *standing still, facing them.*

GANT. It's an appalling situation I know. It's indefensible.

BILL. And so now you are going to try to defend it.

GANT. Absolutely not. I have just taken over the department and what do I find? I was expecting it to be bad, even very bad, but what I've been greeted by is literally indescribable.

MICK (*out of corner of his mouth*). I can describe it.

GANT. I don't think it's possible for me to exaggerate the incompetence I have found here.

MICK. At least he's realised that much.

GANT (*with surprising intensity, back at him*). Of course I've realised it. (*Moving, animated.*) Would outsiders ever believe what goes on here? The main government agency for research and development – you know we now have actual first refusal on discoveries and inventions pioneered in our universities, yes, all the time we have so many different people coming to us – and what have we done? What do we do?

BILL. You do fuck all. That's what you do.

GANT (*unblinking*). Fuck all. Precisely. (*Straight back at him.*) There are no fucking decisions taken if it can possibly be helped.

BILL (*watching him*). And no risks are ever taken.

GANT (*loud, animated*). No risks at all. That's right! Not even small ones. It's like they are forbidden by edict. And things take so long here.

BILL. People publish their discoveries rather than try to market them.

GANT (*loud*). That's absolutely right!

BILL (*forceful, testing for his reaction*). . . . Because at least they get some recognition that way, who can blame the bastards? And a whole range of inventions escape abroad to be gleefully picked up by others, who can't believe their luck. It's –

GANT. It's unforgiveable. And it has to be stopped. (*Straight at BILL.*) Doesn't it! You know we were founded to prevent them escaping and yet they are going all the time. (*Tone changes.*) The things we have lost, some genuinely great ideas. When I think of them . . . (*With feeling.*) the sheer *waste*. (*Suddenly really animated.*) And can you believe the patent system we've still got!

BILL (*warming to this*). The worst in the world, without doubt. It's one of my favourite topics.

GANT (*to MICK*). It can take six years for you to get the patent for your ideas – at least – six years! By which time somebody abroad of course has done it already.

MICK. But we're talking about this organisation – and this organisation is no better.

GANT (*sharp*). No you're wrong. (*Straight at them both.*) We're worse in fact. Considerably worse. We have *one man* to judge all the private inventions that come flowing in here, to decide if we proceed with them or not, how can he be an expert in so many subjects? I have no idea – (*He smiles.*) nor does he. (*Pointing at MICK.*) You know this boy was incredibly lucky to get past him, less than one in a thousand do.

BILL. And look what good it's done him.

MICK. None – worse than none!

GANT. So far. Remember I'm here now. (*Loud sharp.*) Please remember that.

BILL (*sceptical*). So you're going to really change things are you? Looking round here, this miserable set up, it certainly doesn't look like the nerve centre of research and development.

GANT (*with feeling*). I know, I know. I've been thinking about it a lot recently, it hits you very quickly. Outside the streets are alive are they not, the new music, the new clothes (*Sharp smile.*) like you're wearing, the city is vibrant, the country is vibrant out there, but up here, in these rooms high up here we . . .

BILL. You should be part of all that. What's happening out there.

GANT (*really animated*). That's it. Exactly. We should, this should be one of the most significant places, because we're not ephemeral, we're about the future, ideas that will last – but instead we are a complete shambles and nobody outside realises it! Inventions landing here and drying up, dying in fact. They are. Because there isn't anybody here who will take the chance. Till now. I have to be able to change that. (*Looking at him.*) *We* have to.

Slight pause.

MICK. He's bullshitting – this is just to stop us making trouble. He knows this is what we want to hear.

BILL (*dangerous smile*). That's more than possible.

GANT. If it wasn't such a pleasant autumn evening, I would resent that. (*Loud, with surprising passion.*) Do I sound like a normal civil servant, does this seem like the usual crap you get from them? Am I what you expected? (*Looks at both of them.*) I have just taken over this place, and I'm still young (*Self-mocking smile.*) rumour has it, and if I survive in this job, *if*, it will soon be unrecognisable round here. I will make it happen Mr Galpin. (*Pointing at the boy.*) And his ideas which I happen to know are good, one of them is breathtaking in fact, are going to be a top priority.

BILL. They better be.

GANT. Yes, we need somebody to help develop them with us, your interest is just what I want. (*Looking at* BILL.) There are such possibilities now. I can tell you, I've been watching what you've been saying and doing on the media, trying to galvanise support for innovation, reaching out, I really admire that. You are attempting to become a significant patron for new ideas, that's a wonderful notion, don't for godsake stop, you've only just begun!

BILL. Absolutely, I've only just begun, you don't have to tell me that.

GANT. We need people like you, I need people like you, out there, working on the outside, giving a lead. (*With intensity.*) Please, please, whatever you do, whatever happens, don't *stop*.

Blackout.

Burst of sixties pop music mixed with electronic bleeps and other noises.

Scene Five

Spot on ROXANNA *in virginal white wedding dress, standing in spot front stage – as the lights on the main set come on gradually behind her.*

ROXANNA. August 17th – I think it's my wedding morning.

Sometimes you do things that seem truly crazy – to a lot of people anyway . . . including yourself.

DANNY *and* FRANCES *on main set,* FRANCES *draping flower decorations over the great packed heaps.* DANNY *is setting up a row of three machines along base, cylindrical but slightly stocky tubes.* ROXANNA's *shoes and belt, lying on floor.*

ROXANNA *turns, throws her veil back.*

I feel extremely sick.

FRANCES. Natural on your wedding day – you've got to throw up at least once.

ROXANNA (*pulling at dress*). It's like being coated all over in icing sugar – how did I end up doing this?

DANNY. Because you know it's the only way he'd let you get married.

ROXANNA. Oh really, (*Pointing at heaps.*) like this you mean! He's doing it in yet another new house, but he hasn't bothered to unpack!

DANNY. Of course he hasn't – because he'll be moving again, in another few months.

FRANCES (*by heaps*). At least he's taken the plastic wrappings off some of this in your honour!

DANNY. He can't settle anywhere – he's constantly on the move.

ROXANNA (*up to cylindrical machines*). And what are these? I still haven't found out what they are.

DANNY. I think they are some new sort of heat pump.

ROXANNA. Heat pump!

DANNY. Filtering air from outside, or converting or – I don't know, you'll understand it better than me.

ROXANNA. They're all over the place. (*Touching pumps.*) This is truly eerie isn't it – sharing my wedding reception with heat pumps. Pride of place going to the miniature kidney machines, yes have you seen, prototypes of dwarf kidney machines on display right next to the wedding breakfast – they are practically sitting in the bowls of chicken mayonnaise. (*She looks around.*) It's wonderfully vulgar . . .

FRANCES. Of course, you don't expect him to miss a chance like this, to display his likeliest projects, have his wares on show. (*Slight smile.*) And he thought it would be an original touch.

DANNY. Even the musicians are having to play on new lightweight instruments, Roxy, the innovation players, a sort of perspex music, (*Sharp smile.*) only kidding.

ROXANNA (*by heat pumps*). I dread to think what I'm going to get as a wedding present.

DANNY. He has an extraordinary eye for projects at the moment doesn't he – of course a lot of them may not show a return for some time. (*Nervous smile.*) I have to tell him about my new job . . .

ROXANNA. He won't want to hear what *I've* got to tell him . . .

DANNY. He won't approve about this job, he never does, I don't mind, I'll exaggerate the salary if he asks. If only I didn't get so tongue tied when I talk to him, I splutter like an idiot, or suddenly become really leaden, just say the most stunningly obvious things all the time! He shouldn't have that effect on me still.

ROXANNA. Why are we talking about him? I'm the one meant to be getting married and it's getting really close. (*Then immediately turns to* FRANCES.) Who's he bringing today – which of his many girls?

FRANCES. Could be any of the current six – or all six at once of course. He's been Hoovering them up at the moment, girls, just recently.

ROXANNA (*lightly*). Dad only needs a little casual sexual refreshment, a quick snack, it probably only lasts a few minutes with him, and then he's off again alone, working for another six months.

BILL *enters.*

ROXANNA (*without a break*). Did you hear that?

BILL (*straight back at her*). All of it, yes.

DANNY. Hi Dad – you look great.

BILL *in elegant summer suit.*

BILL. Thank you, Danny.

DANNY. And this is all terrific – nobody has ever had a wedding like this, I shouldn't think!

BILL. Clearly. (*Looks across.*) It suits you Roxanna, the dress.

ROXANNA. No it doesn't – I feel ridiculous.

BILL. I was joking, I never thought I'd see you looking like that.

ROXANNA. Neither did I. I suppose I did it to please you. (*Self-mocking smile.*) Extraordinary as it may seem.

> ROXANNA *puts a belt on – a red snake round her on top of the otherwise totally white dress.*

BILL. That's much better – that's more like you, isn't it.

DANNY. I have a new job Dad – the one I wanted, at a good firm, Johnson Fulbright, isn't that great news.

BILL (*ruffling* DANNY's *hair*). Well done Danny.

DANNY (*nervous, loud*). It is good isn't it! Better than I thought, they do the accounts for many leading firms, I knew you'd be pleased, half pleased, aren't you?

BILL. It's good Danny. It's fine.

ROXANNA. Don't be so grudging.

DANNY. He's not being, he's not!

FRANCES (*finishing, arranging heat pumps*). So I've done the heat pumps, and the kidney machines, (*Animated.*) that just leaves the super twist liquid crystal display – simple. (*She moves off, abrasive smile.*) OK. I'll expect something for this, extra champagne at least. (*She exits.*)

DANNY (*following her, loud*). I'll help you – this is going to be a wedding that nobody is ever going to forget, I'm sure . . . (*He exits.*)

ROXANNA (*tightening her red snake belt*). So why am I having such a weird wedding reception, Dad?

BILL (*light*). I suppose I thought it would amuse you. Extraordinary as it may seem.

ROXANNA. A wedding full of prototypes! So are all the guests going to be oddly shaped boffins?

BILL. I knew you'd hate a conventional wedding.

ROXANNA (*suspicious*). Is that the real reason?

BILL. Of course. (*Sharp smile.*) You're always saying how old-fashioned I am – in everything but my work – I'm sure people will think this deeply trendy.

ROXANNA (*wary smile*). Oh yeah? Christ knows what Charlie will make of it.

BILL *looks blank for a second.*

Charlie, you know, the man I'm about to marry, my husband . . .

BILL. Oh him! He'll understand. (*He moves.*) I want to tell you about some of the things here – I'm beginning to shift from ideas that . . .

ROXANNA. Dad no. I knew that's why you were doing this! (*Staring straight at him.*) I think you should move several feet from anything breakable right now, go on, because I've got to tell you something. (*Looks at him, then away.*) I'm going to art college. I'm giving up everything else. I'm not doing what you want.

Momentary silence, she stares at him nervously.

Yes, I know, I'm being very predictable aren't I, thinking I can paint, going around smelling of dope, barefoot in the street, slogans on the wall, it's very ordinary I know. (*Loud.*) But I'm doing what I want.

Slight pause. She smiles.

Go on scream at me, tear up the floorboards. (*Defiant smile.*) Whatever you try, I can handle it.

Momentary pause.

BILL. You'll never be any good.

ROXANNA (*combative smile*). That's nice and subtle for an opener! You don't know that at all, you know I've always been good at drawing.

BILL. Not that kind.

ROXANNA. You've never seen anything else I've done.

Slight pause.

BILL (*briskly, watching her*). Right!

ROXANNA (*circling*). Is that it! Is that all I am going to get? I'm looking for a real fight, come on Dad, aren't I going to get it?

BILL. It's your wedding Roxanna. (*Watching.*) You've chosen the day very cleverly, to tell me. We can't fight on your wedding.

ROXANNA. Can't we. It's today or nothing.

An alarm goes off, loud and bleating.

Jesus, what the fuck is that?

BILL (*smiles*). Oh just a new form of burglar alarm I'm thinking of backing, that's the prototype, the guests will constantly set it off this afternoon as they come in.

ROXANNA (*warm, straight back*). At least it'll drown the speeches then – including yours for once.

BILL. I'll show you how it works in a minute. (*Moving towards her.*) These are exciting times you know Roxanna.

ROXANNA (*straight back*). Oh I know that! It's my wedding.

BILL. – and all that knowledge you've got has to be kept ticking over.

ROXANNA. It's childhood knowledge that – it's going . . .

BILL. You'll find you can't get rid of it.

ROXANNA. Can't I? – I've managed to forget the makes of all the cars you taught me, on those walks as a kid.

BILL. I'll give you a test and we'll see.

ROXANNA (*watching him, moving slightly as he gets close*). You know when we got to the park on those walks, because I was always so excited being with you, I used to imagine the pond, instead of having boring old ducks in it, was full of a dynamic subterranean filter system, with superbly engineered new pipes, twisting around, doing wonderful things. (*Right up to him.*) So we're declaring an armistice are we, you and me?

BILL. Maybe . . . yes.

ROXANNA (*lightly*). Do I trust you? (*Wary.*) I expected you to attack harder. Your tie needs retying. (*She begins to do it.*) Otherwise you don't look bad at all, almost elegant. (*As she ties*

tie.) I'm more than a little worried about what *you're* doing
you know.

BILL (*surprised*). What *I'm* doing?

ROXANNA (*lightly*). Yes, some of it could be good, although I
wish you were a little more socially aware, to put it mildly,
gave something to charity for a start.

BILL. I do!

ROXANNA. Not enough. (*Stronger.*) And you have to be careful
you're not backing too many things, spreading yourself over
too many areas.

BILL (*surprised*). First you tell me I'm going to seed, now you say
I'm doing too much.

ROXANNA (*forcefully*). And you don't delegate.

BILL (*really loud*). You're *always* telling me to do that – you used
to yell from your cot 'delegate, delegate, for chrissake delegate
some more!'.

ROXANNA. You don't know how to, that's your problem. And
you're bombarding people too much at the moment, you're
always popping up somewhere with your ideas.

BILL (*amused smile*). I'll tone some of it down then.

ROXANNA. Yes, I don't want you making too many enemies – a
few is good of course.

BILL. So – my little girl . . . always giving advice.

ROXANNA (*animated, energised*). That's right – your 'little girl'.
Got any normal parental advice for her on her wedding day,
about sex maybe. 'Get enough of it, make sure he satisfies
you.' (*Sharp smile.*) Actually he's above average in that
department, good, solid performer. (*Looks at him.*) I don't see
why *I* should give all the sound advice around here . . .

BILL. Since you ask, since you want to know.

ROXANNA (*loud, immediately moving away*). That was really
stupid of me wasn't it – no don't say what you're about to,
OK, don't you try to –

BILL (*cutting her off*). Would I tell my only daughter not to get married 50 minutes before her wedding?

ROXANNA. Yes you would – no doubt about it at all.

BILL. Then I will. You shouldn't do this Roxanna – I can't put it any other way. He's not right for you.

ROXANNA (*furious*). Jesus!

BILL. And you don't really want him either.

ROXANNA. I wondered when your real assault would come, you think he's influencing me away from what I should be doing – is that it – you're completely *wrong*.

BILL. No – I think you want to be part of what I'm doing, this is not like trying to force one's kid to do something they don't want, quite the opposite.

ROXANNA *looking at him.*

For some reason at the moment you won't let yourself – but this guy is not going to make you happy Roxanna, I promise you.

ROXANNA. Oh yes he will, everything is always so screamingly obvious to you isn't it, you feel you can just beam in on my personal life for a few minutes, and know all about it.

BILL. I think about you quite a lot, more often than you will ever guess. (*Calmly.*) And to make you even more furious Roxanna (*Looks at her.*) – I'm usually right aren't I?

ROXANNA (*shouting*). No, not always, no . . . no.

BILL (*softly*). Don't do it Roxanna.

ROXANNA. I'm warning you, stop it for chrissake, just stop it. (*Strong, dangerous.*) You hear.

Pause.

BILL (*quiet*). OK . . . OK.

Music in distance.

ROXANNA. That wasn't funny you know.

BILL. I was only testing.

ROXANNA. No you weren't, that's rubbish, total shit, that's not worthy of you, you were deadly serious and you know it. And you're not going to be able to resist another push, are you? (*Looks at him.*)

BILL (*lightly*). Come here – come on.

ROXANNA. Why?

BILL. I've been taking dancing lessons – I want to try a few steps.

ROXANNA. How typical – the constant 'self-improvement' classes you insist on doing. Hoping to go to society balls are you?

BILL. Maybe.

ROXANNA. You still want that, don't you, to belong to all that! Thrilled at last to be accepted by, which club was it? The Saville?

BILL. The RAC. The Saville turned me down.

ROXANNA (*moving closer*). I bet you took lessons in two sorts of dancing as well, ballroom and tap probably, wasn't it?

BILL. Yes. Totally correct. So we'll dance? Just dance. OK . . . I'll try out my waltz . . . Can even talk about your painting.

They dance.

(*Sharp smile.*) You know I thought you were bright enough to see that things arty are not more glamorous . . . than, say, heat pumps!

ROXANNA (*slight smile, straight back*). I'm quite bright enough – to see that.

BILL (*as he dances*). As I've got hold of you, I'll just tell you a few of the things I'm investing in, a few of the projects I'm backing, and maybe you'll give me your opinion, just for old times' sake, Roxanna?

ROXANNA. I knew it. (*Slight smile.*) There's no way, Dad, I'm coming back, you do realise that. Absolutely no way.

Blackout.

Wedding music continues, fades into the buzz of electric typewriters.

Scene Six

The table and two chairs front stage, GANT waiting, new leaflets and brochures piled high on table, sharp pencils and a large stapler.
    GANT standing stock still waiting for them.
    BILL and MICK move towards him. BILL is wearing same suit as wedding, but with new cashmere coat over it and with another brilliantly coloured lining. MICK is more soberly dressed than in previous scene with GANT.

GANT. Gentlemen – welcome. How terrific to see you . . . I've been expecting you.

MICK. I bet you have.

BILL. Just wait a moment Mick. (*Restraining hand on boy.*) Let's see if we can do this in a civilised way . . . (*Dangerous.*) as far as is possible.

    BILL sits authoritatively, his coat spread out, smoking.

    (*Dangerous smile.*) Something's been happening, something which very rarely happens to me – you haven't been returning my calls . . .

GANT. I haven't been returning your telephone calls! That can't be so. Of course I'd return them – I would be quite mad not to answer calls from somebody like you. (*Making a note.*) There must have been a failure of communication around here. I'll look into it straight away.

BILL (*icily*). You haven't been answering my letters.

GANT. Letters! Ah letters are different – they may have gone to one of my colleagues, they deal with the mail – I'll investigate this personally.

MICK. What shit is this?

BILL. Patience, patience. (*Staring at GANT.*) Do you know how long it is since we three first met?

GANT. A little while – I've been hoping you'd be in touch.

MICK. But he has been in touch!

BILL. Thirty-four months – just roll that around for a moment and feel its length, how does it seem? Is that long enough?

GANT (*calmly*). Thirty-four months, really? Time evaporates doesn't it, vanishes – must be even truer for someone as busy as you are.

BILL. And you know what the funny thing is?

GANT (*surprised*). What's the funny thing?

BILL. You look so well on it – (*To* MICK.) He's positively blossoming isn't he!

MICK (*loud*). He's definitely blossoming yes – while he does fuck all.

BILL (*restraining hand*). Gently, gently. Can you tell me very simply, very directly, what's going on here?

GANT. I can tell you precisely. We've been very busy having to process everything that comes in here, thousands of unsolicited ideas. (*He smiles.*) Mostly in brown paper parcels you'll be interested to hear, in fact for a time you couldn't move round here without stepping on a brown paper parcel. We've been restructuring and now the department is transformed, as you can see. Look at these leaflets you'll . . .

BILL (*straight at him*). You've got this boy's designs and inventions and you are effectively destroying them by doing nothing for year after year, that is criminal – it's not even as if they'd cost that much! There can be no defence for such behaviour.

GANT. No, no, we are not doing nothing. That is totally unfounded. We are waiting, and waiting hard, any day we expect . . .

MICK. Waiting for what for chrissake!

GANT (*to* BILL). Waiting for certain people we have approached about his ideas, people who might develop them with us, to respond. And we're going to hear very soon, all being well.

MICK (*incredulous*). I don't believe this! I just can't.

BILL. Not so loud. (*Staring at* GANT.) Correct me if I'm wrong – but I was under the strange impression that you already had an entrepreneur who was rather eager to commit money to this boy's ideas! A great deal of money, to develop them, either in partnership with you, or to take them off you entirely, for *ever*.

MICK (*loud*). If only you could.

GANT (*to* BILL). And you'll be next, I assure you! You are the very next one on our list. Yes! Without doubt, if these others don't come through, I'm sure . . .

BILL (*moving by small table*). You have turned this place into a mad house you realise.

GANT. Our ways may seem a little strange at the moment, but there is method here, and I'm personally still totally committed to putting an end to the waste of the past, we must take more risks, the situation is crying out for it. (*He smiles.*) You know I'm flattered that a tycoon of such passion and energy and somebody who is investing in a whole range of other ideas, should be spending so much time, is so obsessed with this one.

BILL (*moving*). Obsessed. Did you say obsessed?

GANT. Please don't feel I think you are over-concentrating on it, no, let me say at once, I think you have a very good nose for finding winning ideas.

MICK (*loud, imploring*). Just give me my designs back – OK – just give them back. I'll do anything to get them back!

GANT. No, no we can't do that. We can't return them. I can see true possibilities in them, as you know. They're *major* ideas.

MICK (*shouts*). Jesus! . . .

BILL (*to* MICK *as he moves round desk, bearing down dangerously on* GANT). Don't get angry, that's a mistake, don't raise your voice at him.

GANT. Absolutely. We are after the same thing totally. You are stirring things up and so am I. Every day we take a step nearer making it happen here, backing good projects. I *assure* you I am not just saying this for your benefit. Things are changing at last. I think we'll surprise each other, I do.

BILL (*catching hold of him*). I have that feeling too, I have that feeling really rather strongly, right at this moment.

GANT. I think now I may have a call coming through, I have to take . . .

BILL (*rage controlled, but frightening*). I can see us coming back year after year, and you flapping around this office, waving your hands, shouting 'everything is changing, it really is', becoming a kind of nemesis for us, getting more and more passionate with each fucking visit.

MICK (*alarmed*). Bill, careful –

GANT (*loud*). I have an urgent call about to come through, I can hear it, will you kindly just . . .

BILL *has got him by the tie.*

BILL (*indicating MICK*). He thinks you were always full of shit – but I think for a moment you really meant it. (*Pulling tie.*) You did – and then you got to the brink and decided doing nothing was much easier, for some reason. (*Loud.*) You won't act will you, and that's going to go on and on and on.

BILL *staples him to desk, jabbing down on tie.*

I am not going to let that happen, my friend.

Blackout.

Scene Seven

Applause dying away, as if at the end of a public speech, rustling, buzz of conversation, a slide screen being lowered with spotlight on it, a single microphone on stand in middle of the stage. Frontstage DANNY and ROXANNA, extreme left, on edge of stage.

DANNY smart suit and tie, small hamper at his feet. ROXANNA dressed in black, her voice different, new languid tone. They are passing a bottle of wine between them. ROXANNA's face is like chalk.

ROXANNA. Is he on soon? I don't like this suspense . . .

DANNY. I think any moment – still writing his speech somewhere under the stage probably.

He stares around, holding the bottle, taking a gulp.

It's a weird sight – the whole of the Albert Hall filled with company directors.

ROXANNA (*taking the bottle off him*). I think I'll need several bottles to get through this.

DANNY. You've missed the hamper lunch. (*He smiles.*) Every captain of industry has one each, a hamper to himself, to tuck into.

ROXANNA. Maybe they'll be so full, they'll sleep through his speech, heaving stomachs all round.

Looking at microphone.

Is it going to be embarrassing Danny? He's not going to strut about all over the place is he? – I don't want it to be embarrassing.

DANNY. I don't know, I'm not sure how he'll play it . . . Just so long as he doesn't pitch it to the TV audience. It's not the done thing . . . the people here wouldn't approve.

ROXANNA (*another swig of the bottle*). I never realised that a hall entirely full of managing directors would have such an amazingly pungent smell.

DANNY (*sharp smile*). Cigars lighting up, although all smoking's banned! (*Staring up the side of the proscenium.*) Ash falling on our faces . . . You know I want to be among them, one of them, more than anything else, Roxanna, I admit it. (*Broad smile.*) It's simple, it's all I want . . .

Lights dimming on them, spot brightening middle of stage.

ROXANNA (*with bottle*). What's happening? Is this it?

DANNY. I hope Dad isn't tempted to attack them in any way, it may not go down too well – he's a lot more successful than most of them.

ROXANNA (*as light fading on them*). Where are you? I'm going to hold onto you, in case this is going to be really bumpy.

BILL *enters in spot, in his pale suit, and defiant red and white shoes.*

Danny those shoes – what on earth is he doing in those shoes?

BILL *taps microphone.*

BILL. Afternoon.

Behind him on screen plump face of Victorian gentleman appears.

I want you to take a look at this face, this undistinguished flabby face, usually these are the people that escape for ever, the ones that say *no*. This man is a good friend of mine – Sir William Preece. Who? Precisely, his name hasn't been heard in public for eighty years. (*Barking it out.*) Preece, head of the British Post Office. (*Anarchic smile.*) It could become a new expression 'to Preece', 'preecing' . . .

Slide changes, another view of same gentleman.

In 1873, he turned down Thomas Edison's development of electric light, declaring that it was a 'completely idiotic idea' – in 1876 he turned down the telephone saying it might be all very well for the Americans, but the British had plenty of small boys who could run messages for them . . . Not bad going was it, in the space of three years turning down two of the most important inventions of the nineteenth century and still having time to be chairman of his club's wine committee. (*Staring up at the fat face.*) I have his picture above my desk, and I'll be handing out copies for you at the end – because my contention is we are all Sir William Preeces now, all of us *here*. Maybe he was the beginning of the end, the end of the age of risk.

Slide changes, another view of Sir William Preece's smug face, which continues to stare down during speech.

I am going to use a very filthy word now – a word that shocks and is generally considered obscene, I am an engineer! Yes, an engineer. They will bleep that out of the telecast, it is already erased, otherwise people will be phoning in to complain.

Moving in spot.

Why has that become such an unfashionable, discredited

occupation? (*Glancing around, sharp smile.*) Just look at your reactions, the revulsion up there – we have to promote the idea of the engineer as superstar – to capture the minds of the young (*Close, soft, in microphone.*) . . . and why my friends are we so *afraid*, all of us, businessmen and financiers sitting here on this sleepy Friday, afraid of innovation, of backing it . . . terrified of failure.

Takes microphone off stand, moving, spot following him.

We believe we're progressing don't we, to a hot technological future, but this is an illusion of course because only a tiny fragment of the progress and inventions that are created are *allowed* to happen.

FRANCES *coming on with large basket, moving a little nervously into spot.*

Because for a start we often suppress them don't we? Large corporations for miscalculated business reasons buy up patents and kill the ideas. Simple ideas that could make a difference to all our lives. We all know the example of the ever-lasting light bulb developed some years ago – and suppressed but, by an extraordinary coincidence, I have some here.

FRANCES *with large basket of snowy white light bulbs.*

(*Sharp smile.*) How did I get hold of them you'll be asking? Aren't they beautiful – first time, they've been seen in public for many years, we'll be handing them out at the exit later, (*He smiles.*) to a lucky few. Thank you, Frances.

FRANCES *moves off with bowl of light bulbs, as she passes* BILL, *he plucks one out of the basket.*

(*Looks out, direct, as if they were all personally responsible.*) But far more important than the suppression we go in for – is what we've allowed to escape. We allowed the jet engine to get away of course didn't we, the whole commercial development of penicillin, the computer naturally, even an early form of lego, the most successful toy in history – because *we* just wouldn't back them when they asked us. (*He clicks his fingers.*) Ideas are escaping right this moment as we sit here – and of course because we hate them.

He glances out sharply.

Yes we do don't we, we entrepreneurs. I'm guilty of this, I
freely admit it. We hate the individual inventor, the loner,
who comes arrogantly along with an idea out of nowhere. Ask
any patent agent and he will tell you there is an officially
recognised jealousy factor that inventors must be aware of, the
manufacturer deeply resenting profits accruing to an individual
who dared to come from outside the firm. Some people not in
industry find this hard to believe but we know it's true.
(*Smiles.*) We know we can be jealous bastards.

FRANCES *coming back on, joins him in spot, carrying two rifles.*

I can see people ducking, don't worry, I am not going to shoot
the worst offenders today.

BILL *taking the rifles, one in each hand, holding them, his arms
high.*

Let's take the story of two guns, a very vivid and savage
example of the jealousy factor at work all the way from the
war in Vietnam, you see how far it stretches.

BILL *standing with two guns.*

The M14 and the AR15 – (*Sharp.*) this doesn't get too
technical so don't worry! The M14, (*Waving one gun.*) the
gravel belly is inefficient and unsuited to jungle warfare. Along
comes an outside inventor, that detested animal, with this.
(*Waving other gun.*) The AR15, fully automatic, easily loadable.
Despite huge pressure, the American Army of course won't
take it – but when eventually they are forced to, what do they
do?

He tosses one gun at FRANCES, *moves with the other round
stage.*

So as not to lose face – the jealousy factor – they have to
'develop' and 'militarise' it, which means (*Pulling back catch on
gun.*) it now jams most of the time when it worked perfectly
before, and it has such a big kick (*Moving with gun.*) that if I
took a shot at – Sir William Preece for instance . . . (*Lifts
gun.*) it will probably split my head open. Do I have any
volunteers?

Swings round with gun.

The brutal truth is, the Vietnamese didn't even bother to take these off dead bodies. (*He smiles.*) Usually the J. factor only kills ideas not people. Thank you Frances.

FRANCES *leaves. He has retained one gun. He moves back, close to microphone.*

(*Direct, incisive.*) People are *not* getting the technology they deserve I'm sure you agree, (*Sharp smile.*) we're not giving it to them, are we? Someone said to me, just last week, all the fun is in computers now, because cars and planes and most machines are a static product. Well computers are beautiful of course and vital and I have put money into them. *But* the motor car has basically not changed in 40 years and pollutes like hell! And of course people are not getting the buildings they deserve either – a particular obsession of mine as you may know, but you'll be spared that right now (*Spins round.*) except I just want to ask how many here have put up a decent corporate building recently? (*Moves across stage.*) Come on anybody? I see no hands, one at the back – we'll all be along later to have a look.

Pause, he stands staring at them.

So . . . you're asking what the hell is he doing about it? If anything!

He makes a signal into the wings.

Can we have them now please . . . (*He looks back at them.*) I'm attempting in a relatively small way to back individuals and groups with original ideas who have a real excitement about the future and I hope a lot of you will join with me this afternoon.

FRANCES *and* MICK *come on from either side of stage, wheeling on scale models about the size of a child's pedal car, of a road-rail vehicle, a stocky craft with a dynamic and startling pointed nose. They arrange the vehicles around* BILL.

One never knows where knowledge will strike from does one – where ideas will be born. And here is an example.

Moving the boy into the spotlight.

This is Mick, a mechanical engineer and inventor of brilliance, possibly genius, who has designed this rather magical craft, his very latest idea. Like nothing you've ever seen before. (*Sharp smile.*) These are scale models of course, next time I'm here I'll bring the real thing! This is a road-rail vehicle, that can run on roads and very rough roads at that, and then move straight onto rails and then back again, effortlessly, retracting one pair of wheels like retracting claws.

In the Third World, over large portions of the globe this will have a vital use, revolutionise transport, for it can go up mountains and down sheer valleys, no longer will land have to be flattened, forests cut down, hugely expensive tunnels built. It combines the adaptability of the landrover with the power and grace of a train.

Moving with craft, wheeling it along stage.

Feast your eyes on this craft, it is a simple and world beating idea, and I am going to build it. Who will join me today on this great adventure? (*Brisk.*) Thank you.

Blackout.

Scene Eight

Music behind her, ROXANNA *is standing in spot front stage in her dark clothes winding a dark scarf around her neck, her head half turned away, as if from the light. Her voice has a new, languid, slightly stoned, drawl. Half-way through speech she watches the boy,* MICK, *lifting the models of the road-rail craft and putting them on a pile in the half light.*

ROXANNA. September 8th. Heavy days . . . and nights . . . curtain drawn, hot little room, claustrophobic, dark, shutting out everything, even on the brightest mornings. (*She turns.*) Certainly tasting things I've never tasted before . . . having to struggle through a sea of mess on the floor to get to anything – including my husband. Dirty sticky sheets, old joints floating in the coffee cups – and me curled up . . . in this tight little black ball . . .

ROXANNA *turns as lights up on main set, moving in the dark coat, shoulders hunched, face pale. The models being thrown on the pile, suitcases being shut, sheets being folded, exuberant sense of movement, of imminent departure, clothes and old possessions being collected up.* FRANCES *strapping boxes and slapping labels on the suitcases.* DANNY *moving things,* MICK *sitting on top of the great pile.*

DANNY (*staring at* ROXANNA's *white face*). What's happened to you?

ROXANNA. A rough night, that's all.

FRANCES. Looks like one of several to me.

ROXANNA. One of several hundred more like – life's so busy you see. (*Touching the packed objects.*) So he's off again – never can keep still can he!

MICK *on top of pile, walking along, collecting various items he wants.*

MICK. Yes – we're off! It's incredible isn't it? – He's really going to build this, (*Holding model.*) a prototype and then a whole network over hundreds of miles, we're going to Africa.

ROXANNA (*startled*). To Africa . . . I didn't realise.

MICK. Oh yes – and you know he's done this Albert Hall speech again about my designs, he's high-jacked several more occasions to do it.

ROXANNA (*dryly*). Played other gigs has he? (*Looking at model with professional eye.*) The wheels are a clever mechanism, but I think this machine has a perverse shaped front, this nose – it doesn't need to look like that, this is showmanship rather than streamlining.

DANNY. I'm still recovering from the Albert Hall, you could feel the resentment slowly growing stronger and stronger during Dad's speech – couldn't you?

FRANCES (*bustling with luggage*). No, because I was numb with terror, being made to go on stage and face all those managing directors. (*Laconic smile.*) A rotten audience too . . .

DANNY (*incisive*). There is something wonderful isn't there Roxy, comic even, in a person being *right* all the time, and people know he's right, but he appears so fucking rich at the moment – they hate him for it. They loathe Dad – and so they don't listen to a single bloody thing he says.

ROXANNA. Yes, a rich man who prophesies – who needs it! (*She moves.*) The worst possible combination.

DANNY (*sharp*). The more he does, the more they detest it. Especially as it seems to all come so naturally to him, everything, his instinctive taste about which innovation to back. (*Looks at* MICK.) Up to now anyway! The *money* . . . which he then says he doesn't care about.

MICK. They hate him – but they can't do anything about it! And his commitment is total. That's the great thing, he actually rings me in the morning and asks humbly if it just might be possible for him to come and see *me*.

MICK *with a bundle of things from pile, stuffing them into his bag.*

ROXANNA (*suddenly sharp.*) What are you doing with those things?

MICK. Oh he said come and collect what you want.

ROXANNA (*very sharp*). Did he indeed?

MICK. So I am . . . I've got a new flat to furnish.

DANNY. He's put many of his prodigies into first-class accommodation you see.

FRANCES. The very best working conditions. (*Sharp, to* MICK.) I hope they appreciate it.

ROXANNA. How very considerate of him. (*Swings round, loud at* MICK.) Those are my things you're taking you realise, you've even got some of my childhood books for chrissake – put them back at once!

MICK. Oh really – these are yours are they?

DANNY. And mine too.

MICK. I'll leave them – sorry. He said take *anything* you want. I've got to get another bag anyway.

Moves to exit.

You know your father's great – I thought I was a little sideshow, something he'd pick up and then drop just as quickly when he got bored, but I'm not! He's prepared to spend millions on it. (*He exits.*)

ROXANNA (*loud, to* DANNY). Is Dad trying to punish us, is this what this is about? (*Turns.*) Punish *me* anyway – is it?

DANNY. I'm not sure what he's doing.

ROXANNA (*furious*). It's really petty. (*Rattling suitcase keys.*) I ran things here once, after all.

FRANCES. He asks about you a lot Roxanna.

ROXANNA. Does he? Probably hoping to hear my marriage has disintegrated. And how are we coping Frances, with him, with all of this?

FRANCES. Me? I'm okay. It's exciting in many ways.

ROXANNA. In what way?

FRANCES. Moving with his ideas, following his projects, being close to it all. It's strange sometimes, but interesting. I spend my life now, long days, fielding his calls. He won't take any – unless they're from his prodigies, because he's only interested in their special projects, nothing else.

ROXANNA *moves over to pile of belongings, starts burrowing amongst them.*

ROXANNA. Jesus, I'd better find everything that belongs to me, before it's too late. You too, Danny.

DANNY *moving over.*

ROXANNA. There I am living in a filthy rat hole behind King's Cross Station, and Danny's not much better, are you?

DANNY. That's right, no.

ROXANNA. And there he is playing the great patron, making all this noise about discovering talent, trying to coax their ideas into existence by pampering them in a truly embarrassing fashion. Come on Danny, bring some boxes.

DANNY *and* ROXANNA *move urgently, finding their things, packing them away in boxes, old battered suitcases, which they empty, so they can put their things in them.*

DANNY (*as he does this*). This road-rail vehicle, Roxy will cost some colossal figure – he couldn't find anybody to come in with him, they wouldn't touch it, so he's doing it all on his own! He's either being extraordinarily clever . . .

ROXANNA. Or it's one gigantic ego trip.

DANNY. That's right, you know he's gone into property now?

ROXANNA. Property too, that figures.

DANNY. But not normal property, oh no, he's gradually acquiring a site, bit by bit, along the river, so he can build this hugely ambitious housing scheme using entirely new materials, and a so-called 'Invention Park' – Yes! – To show off his prototype . . . he's going to have all these machines buzzing around by the river.

ROXANNA *shutting bulging suitcase, strapping it shut.*

DANNY (*moves*). I want to be able to tackle him about what he's doing, but I find it so difficult still. (*Turning.*) He's spending so much Roxy, if he goes on at this rate – I mean it can't last for ever – he could easily go broke.

ROXANNA (*very startled*). Broke? . . . Really?

DANNY. Not immediately, but when –

BILL *enters, his jacket draped over his shoulders.*

Dad! We were just wondering where you were.

BILL (*warm, to* ROXANNA). So you decided to come after all Roxanna.

ROXANNA (*drawn towards him despite herself*). Yeah – I nearly didn't make it.

ROXANNA *changes, becomes animated as soon as he's there, sparring with her.*

BILL. You look like you're in mourning.

ROXANNA. You couldn't be further from the truth.

BILL. What's that mean? (*He grins.*) She's not, is she? You're not pregnant are you?

DANNY. Don't look at me – she never tells me anything.

ROXANNA. Not at the moment, wrong again.

BILL. I haven't seen you since the Albert Hall, what did you think? (*Surprised.*) People were enraged apparently, have you seen the papers?

ROXANNA. Has there been anything? I try not to read about you.

BILL. ' – Anarchic businessman lectures the captains of industry like they were a bunch of six-year-olds.'

ROXANNA. That's true for a start, you did.

BILL. I'm told I showed utter contempt for them.

FRANCES. I liked the bit about how he thinks of himself as a mixture of Isambard Kingdom Brunel and Billy Graham.

BILL (*lightly, fast*). I'm also meant to be intensely crude, impulsive and have impossible illusions of grandeur, the road-rail vehicle is a reckless imbecility, far from backing brilliance I'm funding eccentrics and losers (*Slight smile.*) and will become a laughing stock.

ROXANNA (*straight back*). Seems rather mild in the circumstances. (*She moves up to him.*) I've told you many times don't pay attention to what's being said about you.

BILL. If you don't read about me – how do you know?

ROXANNA. I know what some people think of you – you should be pleased they're talking about you, that's all.

BILL (*watching her*). One has to be aware of how one's regarded.

ROXANNA (*strong*). Why? What do you want their approval for, for fucksake? It shouldn't concern you at all.

BILL (*slight smile*). Of course Roxanna, I'll try to remember that.

ROXANNA (*loud*). I mean it. I don't know why I'm giving you free advice anyway.

BILL (*gently, closing in*). It's unstoppable, that's why.

ROXANNA *moving away.*

ROXANNA. Not any more. It isn't anything to do with me any longer. I forgot for a moment that's all. (*Tone changes, very sharp.*) Why are you giving away our things?

BILL. What things?

DANNY. There's been a muddle about some of the things –

ROXANNA. We had as kids, that belong to us. (*Straight at him.*) When we three were together remember, and you're letting anybody that walks in here take them.

BILL. That was a mistake obviously, I didn't mean that to happen.

DANNY. I knew it was only a mistake.

FRANCES (*trying to defuse situation*). Of course, and are you sure you've got everything now that belongs to you?

ROXANNA (*cutting in*). Trying to demonstrate something to us are you?

BILL. I told you it was a misunderstanding, for some reason Roxanna you want it to be more . . . we've been trying to contact you for weeks.

ROXANNA. Oh really – so what stopped you?

BILL. You never answer my letters.

ROXANNA. I tried ringing you, you wouldn't take my calls, you were permanently in a meeting, (*Louder.*) all my childhood you were in a meeting, but you always took my calls, always.

BILL (*lightly*). Yes, I remember your little voice jabbing out, in the middle of the financial crises.

ROXANNA. So you're trying to wipe Danny and me out of the picture? Is that it, disowning us?

DANNY (*sharp*). I'm sure it's not Roxy . . .

BILL. Don't be ridiculous. I'm just getting rid of all of this, because I'm moving again and going away too on this long visit to Africa.

ROXANNA (*looking across all the luggage*). It's like a missionary
setting out, isn't it?

BILL (*forceful*). I'm going to be able to start building the first ever
road-rail network, this is the biggest project I've had Roxanna.

ROXANNA. Clearly. Every time you've moved house so far it's
been because you've backed something important. (*Quiet, to
herself as she turns.*) Not this time.

BILL. I wish you'd spare a few weeks to come and see, watch the
progress, see it grow, nothing more.

ROXANNA. *No.* I can't and you know I can't, *OK*.

DANNY (*quiet, slight smile*). I'd come.

BILL (*homing in on her volatile manner, tone changes*). What's the
matter with you Roxanna?

ROXANNA. Who said anything was the matter?

BILL. You look so pale my love, where's Charlie?

ROXANNA. Who?

BILL. Your husband. (*Mischievous smile.*) Wasn't he called Charlie,
where is he?

ROXANNA. Oh him. At home. And he's still called Charlie. And
before you ask, everything's fine, more than fine.

BILL. Good. (*Up to her, touching her.*) And those aren't bruises are
they, that you've covered with make-up? Caked here . . .

ROXANNA (*moving away*). No, of course not. Jesus that was
cheap, a typically coarse suggestion. I told you everything's
really good. (*Really sharp.*) Better than you can possibly
imagine.

DANNY. Please come on you two, I hate it when you fight. Just
leave it there, OK.

FRANCES (*unfurling sheet*). Yes, you've all got to help me with the
packing, not getting off that lightly, come on.

BILL (*cutting in*). And that's the truth Roxanna? (*Looks at her.*) I'm
glad then.

ROXANNA. Are you? (*Circling him.*) Now you're going to say – so what the hell have you accomplished, what do you do with yourself all day?

BILL (*straight back*). No, I don't need to know.

ROXANNA. No. (*Savage, mocking.*) Come to think of it, you're probably paying for 'research' to be done on me, people outside my window, under the street lamps watching for the first sign that you're going to be proved right, so you can move in, start reconstructing me.

BILL. Fine, Roxanna, right . . .

BILL *is moving to exit.*

ROXANNA. Where are you going? We have some business to do.

BILL (*turning in exit*). Business?

ROXANNA. I thought that might interest you.

Slight pause.

I want some money.

BILL *looks at her.*

A lot of money . . .

BILL. I see (*Quiet.*) If you need some, of course. I thought you always said –

ROXANNA. It couldn't matter less what I've always said.

DANNY (*to* ROXANNA). You should leave this for later – don't do this now.

BILL. Quiet Danny. You want it so you can really get away, is that it? From this, from me . . . ?

ROXANNA. No, you're wrong again. I don't want it all for myself. I want to be able to help the friends I've got, artists, with their music, painting, what you'd regard as all that shit, spend it on my project. (*Straight at him.*) I want some of your money before it all goes.

BILL (*dangerous.*) Before what?

ROXANNA. You heard – before you spend it all. Waste it.

FRANCES. Roxanna, don't do this, it really upsets me, please don't.

DANNY. Yes, stop it Roxy, don't push this now, this isn't the way.

ROXANNA (*moving, looking at* BILL). I don't believe in your present schemes, some of them may be of mild interest, no more, others are just fanciful. At first I thought if he has to be a tycoon, he might as well be a reasonably useful one. But that's changed. It's absurd vanity to think you, all by yourself, can make any difference to investment in new ideas.

DANNY. Roxy, this is not what you should be doing, not now, please, please.

ROXANNA. Most of this will fail, the housing project too. You're destroying your chance of doing something worthwhile, squandering it on the wrong things, on ideas that now have to be so ridiculously grand and long-term, which will lead nowhere. I'm sure we're never going to see the result of most of this . . . we're not –

BILL (*loud, furious*). That's enough Roxanna, don't you talk to me like that you understand.

Catches her by the wrist, pulls her close, as if he's going to hit her.

Because you know nothing about it now, *do you*. As you said you've forgotten it all – so don't you try to tell me anything, any more. Is that clear . . .

Pause.

(*Quieter, close, holding her*). Not a word out of you.

Slight pause.

ROXANNA (*quiet, defiant*). No. (*Being held close.*) So you're going to hit me, to show how right you are, are you?

Pause. BILL *looking down at her.*

BILL (*calmly, slight smile*). Not today . . . not now.

He lets her go, moves, takes out his cheque book, begins to write.

(*Slowly, as he writes.*) Since my daughter feels there will be nothing left – she better have it now.

Tears cheque out, gives it to her, moving.

FRANCES (*quiet*). Roxanna, this is shameful.

ROXANNA. This is not enough. (*Slight pause.*) Double it . . . at least.

DANNY (*to* ROXANNA). What are you doing for chrissake? Just stop this will you, now.

BILL (*staring at* ROXANNA). Fine. Do you want to dictate the amount. Come on Roxanna . . . I'll just write.

Silence.

ROXANNA (*very still*). I'll dictate. If you want. 'September 17th 1973, the city is surprisingly quiet, a sullen grey afternoon, a few days before my entrepreneur father is setting out on his great engineering adventure, . . .'

DANNY (*quiet*). What kind of cheque is this?

ROXANNA. . . . 'to my misguided ex-daughter Roxanna who I may not see for a little while (*Momentary pause.*) the sum of twenty thousand pounds.'

Pause.

BILL. There's a signed cheque, fill it up. I have no interest in how much. I don't expect we'll be referring to this again – Frances, come on, we have a great deal of work to do.

FRANCES *moves after him. Before they have exited* ROXANNA *calls out.*

ROXANNA. Dad – I don't know why it came out like that . . . why I said . . . (*Sharp.*) OK – I don't know . . . because I'm not used to asking . . . or something.

BILL *exits, she follows to call after him.*

ROXANNA. Just one of our normal fights (*Loud.*) wasn't it?

Turning to DANNY.

Danny, wasn't it?

DANNY. I don't know . . . maybe . . . It's like a marriage you two. You fight so hard, there's real blood flying around.

ROXANNA. Still – I got the money didn't I? I can get away now.

She sends a model of the road-rail vehicle rolling across stage.

I can get away from all this – I really can.

Fade.

ACT TWO

Scene One

1983.

ROXANNA *sitting on the pavement/floor front stage, smoking, older, her hair different, wearing a comfortable coat, shopping bags round her.* DANNY *leans against the wall of the stage, the side of the proscenium, ringing an entry phone and then staring up, as if looking up the wall of a building. We can hear a bell echoing inside the building. DANNY is holding a large brown paper parcel, and is smartly dressed, in a fine winter coat, sharp and efficient in appearance, he bristles with a new confidence.*

He is rattling his car keys as he moves, then listens to entry phone.

DANNY. Nothing, absolutely nothing, not even a crackle.

ROXANNA. How many times does that make?

DANNY. At least seven.

ROXANNA. Ring it again, we've hardly started.

DANNY. He was definitely expecting us, I made an appointment for 4 o'clock.

ROXANNA. He's not a great respecter of appointments these days, it just means we should be seen within a week or so.

DANNY. I'm sure he's in there – I saw some movement I think. (*Sharp smile.*) Will you recognise him do you think?

ROXANNA. Don't be ridiculous, I saw him recently.

DANNY. I was only kidding. (*He smiles.*) Half.

ROXANNA. I saw him just before Christmas, or rather a few months before Christmas (*Laconic smile.*) for 20 minutes. He sent the kids presents though, weird modules of some sort.

DANNY. Yes, my kids got the modules too. (*Surprised*.) They loved them. I think they were spaceships that could ski on water – no doubt a new project of his!

ROXANNA (*lightly*). Mind you, I don't think he'd recognise my kids, in fact I'm not even sure he remembers who their father is.

DANNY (*close to her, for a moment*). Are things good between you and Dave at the moment – are you happier?

ROXANNA (*smoking, laconic*). Sometimes yes.

DANNY (*moving, flicking keys*). I'm glad things are more settled with you Roxy, terrific . . .

ROXANNA. That's right.

DANNY (*ringing bell*). Maybe we should throw a few stones. Do you think he's staring down right at this moment, watching us. (*Looking up*.) After his restless moving from house to house settling down in this concrete block is a little weird – (*Turns*.)

ROXANNA (*smoking*). You can just see St Paul's, from one of the top lavatories apparently.

DANNY. *I* haven't seen him for over a year. (*Looking at* ROXANNA.) I haven't grown fatter have I? What do you think?

ROXANNA. A little rounder maybe.

DANNY. Really? You sure? I want to look good when I see him.

ROXANNA. Yes. I worry about that too. It's absurd isn't it.

DANNY. I have a lot to tell him, show him what's going on.

Sudden crackle out of entry phone.

What was that? (*Moving*.) Hello, this is Danny – Danny and Roxanna are here, Danny is outside! Down here. (*Loud*.) We're right outside.

Loud inaudible crackling answer from machine then silence.

Doesn't sound hopeful, does it! That noise hasn't unlocked the door. Either they're all still on the phone –

ROXANNA (*smoking*). – Or he wants to keep us waiting for a good while yet.

DANNY. You're being very calm.

ROXANNA. I smashed the doorknob last time this happened to me – so I thought I'd pace myself this time.

DANNY. Well I've got an appointment in town (*Pushing bell.*) and time is just beginning to be money – (*Sharp smile.*) One of the things I want to tell him. I wonder how his work is really going – what with delays in Africa, because of wars and other minor obstacles.

ROXANNA (*smoking*). And all the time that's gone on the electric car too.

DANNY. There's been a clever mix of small potential money makers and these great projects. (*Sharp.*) He kept that balance going longer than I thought. But the big schemes . . . we must be seeing the results soon, *surely*. (*Moving to machine.*) Can spare him one more ring. I really wanted to give him this.

ROXANNA (*looking at the parcel*). What is that?

DANNY. It's a surprise, but since he's kept us waiting.

He tears off paper to reveal a large virulent caricature painting of his father, dark and twisted like a Francis Bacon, on glossy hardboard.

ROXANNA (*startled*). Jesus, where did you get that?

DANNY. It's a blow-up – I had it done specially, a blow-up of the offending article, the cover, I thought he'd like it. Do you think it'll misfire? (*Sharp smile.*) Could enrage him of course.

ROXANNA (*staring at savage caricature*). There's a slight risk yes.

DANNY. I quite like it (*Sharp smile.*) I don't know why . . . (*Breezy, rattling car keys.*) Are you going to the trial? If they fix a date?

ROXANNA. I expect so, it may be the only chance I have of getting to see him.

DANNY (*lightly*). Yes – you know I think somebody got him to sue for libel, so all the people who want to see him will know exactly where he is on a particular day. (*Looking at* ROXANNA.) Court No.13 probably.

ROXANNA (*quiet*). The rich man's sport. (*Staring at the picture.*) Were there two articles? I could hardly get through this one, it was so boring.

DANNY. I think there were at least two, you know about him having hired some people to force the remaining tenants and little shopkeepers off the river site, because he'd had to wait all these years to build his great housing scheme, that sort of thing.

ROXANNA (*looking at picture*). I should read it obviously.

DANNY (*lightly*). There're a lot of other things of course, how he's totally unqualified to make the judgements and attacks he has, how his ideas are a sham, his crusade for investment in innovation completely bogus, all the usual things! Very unfortunately they have offered to settle out of court – I really hope he doesn't accept, it could be fun.

ROXANNA. Maybe. (*Holding blow-up.*) Can I have this? I think it's probably a better idea to give it to me than to him.

DANNY (*expansively*). Keep it. I knew you'd want one, so I had three made. Mine's already hanging up in the hall, pride of place.

ROXANNA (*sharp smile*). Thanks – I've been looking for a good picture of him to show the kids.

DANNY. Time's up. No more rings. (*Into entry phone.*) If you're there Dad – have to go now – I have another appointment. Catch up with you soon. Your daughter – remember her – wants to say something.

ROXANNA. Yes – I have to get back now to cook for the kids, believe it or not. Bye. (*After thought, flashing out of her.*) And you better bloody not be in there! You hear!

DANNY (*turning as he exits*). He really mustn't settle Roxanna. If he does, we'll never get to see him.

Blackout.

Scene Two

The court environs, large emblem hanging near the back wall, staring down over the action.

There is a long line of seats, belonging to the court passages, front stage, leather high-backed chairs, beginning to split.

BILL, looking hardly any older, is sitting on one of the chairs, talking into a pay phone, he has slightly filled out round the waist, but his movements are full of energy. FRANCES looks distinctly older, tighter, spikier, less relaxed atmosphere to her than in Act One. She's busy with letters, files under her arm, loud buzz of conversation around passage.

BILL (*on pay phone, smiling*). No, no . . . I just wanted to know how you were doing, see if there were any unexpected signs of progress, the progress you keep promising . . . and of course to make sure you're working your arse off, you *almost* are . . . (*He smiles.*) what does that mean? Almost is a word I never use . . . what? . . . Torrential rain. So what's a little rain!

FRANCES (*bristling*). That's quite enough, come on, stop talking, we haven't got long.

BILL. No . . . I can't now. There is a trial apparently about to take place here. Yes I'm right there now.

ROXANNA and DANNY enter. They are out of their coats of previous scene, now in summer clothes.

(*In full flood on phone, doesn't appear to notice them.*) Yes, I've found a faulty telephone box – you know the sort that doesn't ever run out – so I thought I might as well phone Africa . . . of course (*Mischievous smile.*) I'm going to nip out regularly from the court and use it.

ROXANNA. Oh shit – he's on the phone.

DANNY. And then he'll be in court.

FRANCES. And there are two strangers to see you.

BILL (*into phone*). Yes, so you'll move quickly from now on, right?

BILL looking up to see ROXANNA and DANNY, then slight smile into phone.

As you know my patience isn't infinite.

BILL *rings off. He looks up at* DANNY *and* ROXANNA *for a split second not saying anything, then his tone is polite, but dead towards them, indifferent.*

Hi you two – how are you doing?

ROXANNA (*automatically*). Very well.

DANNY. Hello Dad, it's good to see you.

BILL. Yes. (*Immediately turning away to* FRANCES.) How long have we got?

FRANCES. Not long – how many times do I have to keep telling you. (*Bustling around.*) You can't keep a court waiting you realise, and you have a meeting with your legal team first, we ought to be there now.

DANNY (*to* BILL). We'd like to be able to take you out for a meal one day soon. Just for . . .

Phone rings.

ROXANNA. Christ, not the phone again.

FRANCES (*picking it up*). No, he can't take it.

BILL (*spinning round*). Of course he can take it.

FRANCES. Ring back later, he's completely unavailable now. (*Slamming down phone.*) He's only been here a few minutes and he's managed to give out this number to people! (*To* BILL.) And I don't know why you need conduct everything in the passage – we have a room.

BILL. It's full of lawyers, giving me instructions.

ROXANNA (*to* DANNY). Look at that – my hands shaking.

BILL (*suddenly looking at her*). Why? What's the matter? What you shaking for?

ROXANNA. Probably because I'm more nervous than you are.

BILL. About what? About the trial?

ROXANNA. Oh no, not the trial, the trial doesn't matter.

BILL. Doesn't it? I see.

ROXANNA. Of course not, I mean you can handle a small thing like that, I'm much more nervous about this meeting – seeing you again.

FRANCES (*busy, up to* BILL). Come on, I need you to sign these, give me something to do while you're entertaining yourself in there.

ROXANNA. The main excitement is not what you do in the witness box, but trying to catch you for a few minutes in these passages and see what you do then – (*To* BILL, *slight pause.*) isn't it?

BILL (*ignoring her, to* FRANCES). I need to change I think, the other jacket.

ROXANNA (*nervous smile*). Still the same taste in clothes I see, just a tiny bit behind fashion (*Sharp smile.*) but you're closing the gap I think.

DANNY (*as* BILL *puts on jacket*). Getting read for battle . . . You know in olden times if you lost a libel action you had a limb amputated. They literally were damages, maybe a hand, maybe a foot, and in a particularly bad case perhaps a whole leg. (*Jaunty smile.*) People would love to see that now, wouldn't they, entire legs coming off.

BILL. Thank you Danny – that's just what I was hoping to hear before I went in . . . (*Noise from passages.* BILL *smiles approvingly.*) People queueing already I see.

ROXANNA. Looking for a record turnout are you!

DANNY (*sharp smile*). Give people what they want and they turn up etc. etc.

FRANCES (*loud*). We've got to move now.

MICK *enters, as* BILL *moves.*

MICK (*calling out*). Bill – wait! Just came to wish you good luck.

BILL. Jesus – Mick! Look at him! (*With warmth, embracing.*) How fat he's got – encased now, in lard . . . look at this. (*Gives him a playful jab in stomach.*)

MICK. Just older that's all.

BILL. You're not old – you're just beginning still. (*Sharp look*.) Aren't you?

MICK. I'm more relaxed these days, that's for certain.

BILL (*broad smile*). I don't like the sound of that at all. (*To the others*.) You know what he's doing now?

MICK. I wasn't going to tell you that.

BILL (*warm, fast*). But I know! You didn't think I would but I do. This boy has lost his patents, all of them, except the one I've got. The development council let them lapse and he lost out to abroad so what's he doing? Tell them – he's designing parking meters, a new range of parking meters for Scotland. Can you believe that?

MICK. That's roughly right, yes.

BILL. Exactly right. Come with me. (*Warm*.) It's very good to see you you know, maybe we can reawaken something. (*Knowing smile*.) You never know, a few hours with me. I have news about your large baby, the road-rail vehicle, taking shape in elephant country as we speak. (*Sweeping him off*.)

ROXANNA (*loud*). Dad wait.

BILL *stops, she moves.*

ROXANNA. Your tie needs straightening. (ROXANNA *moves up to him. Pause*.)

BILL (*as she straightens his tie*). Don't give me any advice Roxanna, OK . . . (*He begins to exit*.)

ROXANNA. I need to see –

BILL *exits*.

DANNY (*moving after*). Come on! Come on, got to keep up with him.

ROXANNA. You go ahead, OK. (*As* DANNY *exits*.) I need a minute to myself.

GANT *enters briskly*.

ROXANNA. Not him as well. Really! (*She turns away.*)

GANT. Hello. (*Advancing towards her.*) We met once I think at your wedding, which I was lucky enough to attend.

ROXANNA. Oh yes, you were part of the innovation display at my reception, there were more machines than guests I remember.

GANT (*sharp smile*). I think I probably went as a guest (*Looking at* ROXANNA.) I've come to watch your father today.

ROXANNA. I gathered that.

GANT. I'm looking forward to it very much, extremely.

ROXANNA. I bet you are.

GANT. No, no, you've obviously been listening to things he's been saying about me – no I admire your father a lot.

ROXANNA (*sharply*). Really?

GANT. I think he's an extraordinary man – there're two ways of looking at him I suppose.

ROXANNA. Just two?

GANT. An inspired innovator taking risks, evangelical, ahead of his time – or somebody who's just turned into a slightly careless property tycoon . . . I favour the first myself. Yes. (*Moves.*) Have to get a good seat – (*As he exits.*) I'm taking an early lunch all week, so I can catch a bit each day.

ROXANNA (*turning, out front*). July 8th. Not so fast! We're not going in – not yet. I'm not sure I'm going to watch it all. The trial's an irrelevance.

July 9th to 14th. I keep coming back, a grown woman hanging around like a groupie, hoping to get him on his own, and all I get is this bloody trial! Not that I *need* to see him of course, just idle curiosity, and I'll be much too busy soon to keep on trying to see him. (*Tone changes.*) I've been in for a few short doses, and what hits you really strongly, there are no close-ups, you get so used to that from all the TV courtroom dramas, you really miss it, no giant close-ups of Dad, it's really disorientating. And there is no one-hundred-year-old

judge asking 'Who were these men the Beatles?' etc., not in
this trial anyway. Instead there is a very bland, younger than I
expected judge, looking like he's made out of rubber, wearing
a stupid pink sash and with this air of blubbery malice, and
it's so hot in there I keep thinking he's about to melt.

Lights changing behind her.

And Dad has got what he's been hankering for – couldn't do
without – a chance to flex his muscles, to perform in the heart
of the Establishment, in this ludicrous setting, his two-tone
voice ringing out.

And naturally I can't get anywhere near him.

Scene Three

JUDGE, *bland, rubberlike face, sitting high up staring down, wearing
his pink sash and frilly cuffs, in front of the emblem.* BILL *standing in
the witness box, moving restlessly as if the box is too small to hold him,
and then forcing himself to keep still.* QC *moving in front of them,
microphone suspended from ceiling, hanging above* BILL. *He
occasionally almost hits it with his waving arm. Very hot, sticky,
summer light, in two large pools, one round the* JUDGE, *one round*
BILL.

QC. Mr Galpin, it is true is it not that you like to describe yourself
as an engineer?

BILL (*rapid, light*). Yes, I have described myself accurately as an
engineer, you're now going to say (*Very quick smile.*) but I have
no formal qualifications as one, because I did not complete my
training, and the answer to that is . . .

QC. Please don't try to anticipate my questions, that will get
neither us or the court anywhere.

JUDGE *staring ahead.*

BILL (*waving his arm*). I apologise. Ask your questions, I'll answer
anything.

QC. As it happens you were right about my next question, it is

clearly something you are acutely conscious of – you did not
complete your training as a civil engineer did you?

BILL (*rapid, quiet, moving in box*). We are all acutely conscious of
where we have come from, how we began; (*To* QC.) are we
not? I became involved in electrical ideas out of financial
necessity but I did not lose my knowledge of engineering
obviously, you are now going to ask but you have never built
anything have you? The answer to that is literally true,
although it won't be for much longer, some wonderful
buildings are about to . . .

QC. You're doing it again Mr Galpin, you're trying to anticipate
my questions and this time you are wrong.

BILL. Am I?

QC. These matters are obviously right in the forefront of your
mind. Now I hope we won't have to fight over each question,
be involved in a race to see who can get it out first.

JUDGE. Yes, it would help if you didn't try to cross-examine
yourself Mr Galpin, however competent you may prove to be
– try to desist.

BILL. Yes, (*Mumbles.*) my lord. (*Sharp smile.*) I will try to avoid
seeing his questions coming.

JUDGE. And maybe you could do us another favour Mr Galpin
and make a big effort to keep still.

BILL. Keeping still is what I'm worst at. (*Quiet.*) I will try . . .

QC. Nevertheless you are putting my case to the court very well so
far, because one of the issues I want to examine is your
professional qualifications. You have not hesitated in
pronouncing on many public matters Mr Galpin, building,
housing, for instance, and yet you are not an architect?

Pause.

BILL. Sorry, I didn't realise I was meant to reply.

QC. You are not an architect?

BILL. You know the answer to that.

QC. Please do not play to the gallery Mr Galpin, just answer the question please.

JUDGE. I know everybody considers themselves experts in modern architecture these days, but you have never trained as – you are not an architect?

BILL (*glancing around*). No – I am not. Nor am I a fully qualified engineer.

QC. Thank you. I'm glad we've established that. And indeed you made your fortune, your very sizeable fortune, out of a light electrical firm.

BILL. A lot of money, yes.

QC. A great deal of money.

BILL. If you prefer.

QC. And you made this money out of a breakthrough concerning gramophones, and since then you've multiplied your fortune many times. Correct?

BILL (*impatient*). A few times.

QC. And you've been anxious have you not, in the past, to downplay or even to disown this achievement. Why?

BILL (*lightly*). I don't consider it a particularly startling achievement. Once you've got some, any fool can double it.

QC (*sharp*). What did you say? Any idiot can do what?

BILL. No. (*Slight smile.*) Any fool. (*Lightly.*) It's no proof of intelligence, or even any particular skill, quite the reverse in fact in many cases. It was said of my father for instance he was too intelligent to be a rich man. (*He smiles.*) So you see what that says about me. Just to breed money once you've got some is nothing (*Slight smile.*) in my opinion.

QC. I see. And so you have used some of this money to very publicly sponsor a range of miscellaneous inventions?

BILL. Various innovative schemes and designs, yes.

QC. And how many of these varied innovative schemes and designs are on the market at the moment, can you tell us?

BILL. Most are still in development.

QC. How many?

BILL. A couple – I don't want to anticipate your question (*Quick smile.*) and I certainly cannot see it coming, but you are going to want to know a couple out of how many.

QC. Please tell us.

BILL (*lightly*). A couple out of over a hundred – but that is because . . .

QC. Because they're still in development – yes you told us. And some of them have clearly already failed, is that the case?

BILL (*lightly, but incisive*). No, none have failed so far. None. I want to make that clear, (*Slight smile.*) and they're all on schedule despite rumours to the contrary. They are long-term projects. They may take over a decade to come to fruition or more, (*Louder.*) that is why I was interested in them, that is why nobody else wanted anything to do with them. And that is why I decided to spend so much on . . .

QC (*cutting him off*). I see. And you didn't have experts, scientists, or experienced engineers to evaluate what was being offered to you?

BILL. No.

QC. You felt qualified to judge them all, you never delegated, because you have a profound belief in your talent for this – isn't that right?

BILL. If you have found you are reasonably good at spotting potential, you feel confidence in carrying on. You will want to know why in the case of the land acquisition I decided to delegate and . . .

QC. You're doing it again. Not so fast, don't be . . .

JUDGE (*cutting in*). You really must stop asking yourself questions Mr Galpin.

BILL (*giving it an odd emphasis*). Yes, my lord.

QC. You are fond of publicity, are you not?

BILL (*lightly*). No, that's not true.

QC. You are not claiming you are shy of it?

BILL. Nobody's ever called me shy – I admit that, but that's quite different.

QC. I shall rephrase. Over a period of time you have deliberately used your appearances on the media, especially television, for your own purposes?

BILL. Yes, of course. (*Slight smile.*) Doesn't everyone who appears on it do that . . . I wanted to try . . .

QC (*sharp*). I'm coming to that – you wanted to shake up the general approach to innovation and research. Act as a kind of catalyst isn't that so?

BILL. Yes. I wanted to express various ideas. I was certainly not the only one expressing them, but I wanted to broadcast them as widely as possible, popularise . . .

QC. Popularise, exactly. And that is why you sought publicity so avidly. Correct?

BILL. Sought no, accepted yes.

QC. And you 'accepted' opportunities, for instance, if we take a glance at a couple of these ideas, to castigate the record of British management.

BILL. Naturally, no sane person could do anything else, given the opportunity. Initially my interest, (*He smiles.*) my 'obsession', was in how many good ideas we were losing, wonderful notions slipping away, because of our terror of thinking further ahead than tomorrow afternoon, (*He smiles.*) to be deliberately provocative because I don't think it's changed – there's a lack of enterprise.

QC (*sharp*). You say initially this was your obsession.

BILL (*lightly*). Still is very much.

QC. But you underwent something of a conversion did you not about the kinds of ideas you wanted to invest in?

BILL. Yes. I began to see clearly we were over-concentrating on high tech at the expense of low, I've always found high tech products immensely exciting, but they are seducing us away from reality.

JUDGE. For the jury's benefit and certainly for mine, would you interpret that?

BILL (*animated, increasingly confident*). I'm sure they can understand, I can see they do. We're not changing our basic machines – that's what I mean – or building materials, that the ideal existence we are being offered to strive for is a house stuffed with home computers and video recorders and two ridiculously energy-wasteful cars in the drive.

QC. And therefore it has become increasingly important for you to create even more media opportunities for yourself, is that not true, in your campaign for instance to make 'engineering' glamorous again.

BILL (*in full stride*). Yes, that is vital for obvious reasons, because of the imminent collapse, literal collapse of our cities, and the simple question (*He smiles.*) if I'm still allowed to put any questions – who on earth will rebuild them? Because our young are not going into it.

I know from my own children, they turned their backs on all this, especially my daughter who was very gifted. (*He smiles.*) Of this at least I have direct experience, the right qualifications to speak.

But *I* on the other hand have become more and more involved in ideas that engineer our environment in a bold modern way, while helping preserve it at the same time, stopping its wholesale destruction.

JUDGE *moving.*

Do I have your attention my lord, I thought you might have been distracted for a moment? – Like the prototype I have supported of the road-rail vehicle, that's the vehicle with the strange snout some of you may remember, the notorious snouter, whose time has come now (*He smiles.*) I hope, and that will be followed by a new, powerful, and I think commercially viable electric car and then the buildings which –

QC. That's very interesting Mr Galpin. And these are exactly the ideas and projects you wish to popularise at the moment are they not?

BILL. Absolutely – and it's even more important than before, because we've now made it practically impossible for the single individual acting on his own to have ideas commercially accepted, as I'm sure you all know – and if history is anything to go by, we are excluding the very place where real progress has usually come from, (*He smiles.*) from . . . from the left of the field, out of nowhere, ideas that will change our lives, protect our planet –

QC. Right Mr Galpin now . . .

BILL (*carrying straight on*). And of course even when individual brilliance does somehow force its way to the surface, in this country, it's stamped upon, kicked in the teeth, oh yes, because just like the way we select our national sports teams jobbing mediocrity is always preferred to flair, so it is in science and technology, the commercial plodder gets the funding, the unadventurous idea, the one that can show the quick return. (*Lightly.*) And then of course if we are also underfunding our universities it makes –

QC (*loud*). Mr Galpin, please.

BILL *stops*.

I gave you the opportunity to make a speech for a very particular reason.

BILL. I never need a second invitation anyway.

QC. Exactly. That is my point. I put it to you, Mr Galpin, you have a thirst, an absolute compulsion to seek publicity.

BILL (*breezily*). No, that is not true.

QC. But we have just seen it in operation, have we not. We all saw how energised you suddenly became. I put it to you that many of your actions only begin to make sense when this need is understood?

BILL (*lightly*). No, that is not true.

QC. – and I further put it to you that you need publicity very badly precisely at this moment on account of your delayed projects which nobody has yet seen. And that is the main reason for you bringing this action is it not? So it can become a stage, as you've just demonstrated, for you to lecture and promote your views to the court and the press.

BILL. I certainly don't think you can be right about that . . . it's much easier to go on the BBC isn't it? (*Slight smile.*) A lot cheaper too, I believe.

JUDGE (*bland, expressionless face*). I think it could be lunchtime . . .

Blackout.

Scene Four

ROXANNA, DANNY *and GANT, in room downstage, chairs, wall with a few wigs and gowns hanging up, small table, plates of food covered with battered silver bowls. Very hot. Light, intermittent sound of voices from passage.*

　DANNY *moving, rattling car keys.* ROXANNA *smoking in her summer dress, bare sticky arms.*

DANNY (*loud confident*). Come on – come on. Where is he? (*To* ROXANNA.) You know I thought I'd be nervous about this, it's a big surprise but I'm not, I'm fine, I really am . . .

ROXANNA. Are you? I'm not. I'm regressing fast, turning into a jittery little girl which is absurd, because I was never like that as a kid. (*Turning on* GANT.) You realise this is a private lunch.

GANT. Yes – I just wanted to pay my compliments to your father, I think I caught his eye in the passage, I have to see him properly, no question, shake his hand.

ROXANNA. And then get the hell out of here, OK!

GANT. Along those lines, yes. You know we have only met a very few times, your father and me, over the years, and each time not for long, but the strange thing is, hardly a week goes by, without me thinking about him, it's very curious.

DANNY (*sharp smile*). Tell him that – it'll make his day.

GANT. And it's extremely interesting to see him forced to be still isn't it, becuse he's usually always on the move, but to see him like this, under public scrutiny . . . don't worry, I'll be over here.

ROXANNA (*furious*). Jesus. (*Moving across.*) Danny this is going to be ordeal enough, without having to put up with that creep as well.

DANNY (*lightly, putting arm round her*). Calm down Roxy, it's OK. Quite OK. (*Looks at her.*) Things are less intense between you and Dad now, surely?

ROXANNA. Oh yes, only a small bit lingers on . . . if that. It's quite over really.

DANNY (*he smiles*). You're never nervous of anything, are you, anyway?

ROXANNA (*moving*). Dad's going to give me his own cross-examination I know and I have to be ready for it. 'Why you here?' reply 'Because I am!' (*Imitating withering tone.*) 'What are you doing with yourself these days?' (*She replies.*) 'Working three days a week in a bookshop and why not?' 'Spent all the money have you?' 'Yes – and things are pretty good too!'

DANNY. Just be yourself – what's so difficult? That's all that's –

BILL *enters, same clothes as in the witness box, but he's changed his shoes, fashionable footwear. He sees* GANT.

BILL. Ah it's my mate from long ago! (*He smiles.*) Isn't this marvellous – the place is full of enemies.

GANT. I just wanted to say hello.

BILL. It really is like my funeral, all of them uninvited, all of them staring down at me, people I'd forgotten existed coming running up saying 'We are watching you, we're having such a good time!' But this character here (*Indicating* GANT.) is different. (*Points.*) I've only met him a few times, but I've never forgotten him.

GANT (*smiling*). Really? I was just telling them how . . .

BILL (*cutting in*). A taste that keeps coming back. And how are things with you, has anything changed?

GANT. Oh yes, of course. It's a very exciting time, under this government we've changed our name, we have a new title and and we have a smaller staff, cleared out the dead wood.

BILL. *You* survived of course!

GANT. Naturally. (*Smiles.*) That was never in doubt. I've been given extra powers in fact. And we're full of new energy I hope. I'm still passionately committed to improving our success rate.

BILL. Still find making decisions rather tough, do you?

GANT. No, not at all. Looking into the future is never easy of course . . . (*Shrewd look.*) as you know – but for instance we've just moved on a revolutionary process for the manufacturing of a variety of fast foods – beat the Japanese to it for once. You see, I can make decisions! (*Provocative smile.*) Whether that particular project would meet with your approval or not, I don't know. (*Looks straight at* BILL.) How are things progressing with you?

BILL. Steadily, as I'm sure you know.

GANT (*shrewd sceptical look*). Steadily? . . . That must be encouraging. And I expect they will move quicker from now on. (*Sharp smile.*) Most things do. (*He moves.*) I very much like following what you've been doing, that's what I wanted to tell you. Just that. (*Shaking* BILL's *hand.*) Got to go. Of course I'm interested to see how all this turns out. Good luck. (*He exits.*)

BILL (*slight smile, watching him go*). Vermin. The extraordinary thing about him is he's bright enough to see the possibilities in ideas – and he still does nothing. A destroyer.

DANNY. Hi Dad.

BILL. Hello, you two.

Momentary silence. BILL visibly begins to withdraw inside himself, suddenly alone with them, becomes vulnerable.

DANNY. I think it's going great – you are doing very well, excellent.

BILL. Maybe. (*Not looking directly at* ROXANNA.) What do you think?

ROXANNA. You're doing OK. (*Slight smile.*) A little over the top.

DANNY. No, no, it's going fine.

ROXANNA (*warm*). And this room is terrific for us, the territory you've chosen, bits of judges hanging there, to stare at us, must everywhere, lawyers seething outside. (*Laconic smile.*) It couldn't be better. (*Warm.*) Your dream location, isn't it, to be able to eat here?

BILL. Always so impressed by anything institutional aren't you Roxanna. (*Watching her.*) So help yourself to some lukewarm food.

BILL turns to trays of food, he seems more ill at ease than in witness box.

ROXANNA (*suddenly moving right up to him*). I brought some pictures of the two boys, Mark and Nicholas. (*Nervous joky smile.*) Your grandchildren, in case you'd forgotten. Do you want to see?

BILL (*with tray of lukewarm food*). Of course – put them there . . . I'll look at them later.

ROXANNA (*instinctively flaring up*). What's that mean, you'll look at them in a couple of weeks? Look at them now!

BILL. I just had my hands full – I meant I'd look at them in a minute. (*Sharp.*) That's all I meant.

ROXANNA. Here they are. (*Showing pictures.*) Look.

BILL. Yes. (*Quiet, awkward.*) That's a very beady stare they're giving – quite big boys now – it's a long time since I've seen them.

ROXANNA (*pushing the pictures back into his hand*). Don't you want to keep them. (*More urgent.*) Go on, have them.

BILL. Yes. (*Taking the photographs.*) And Danny . . . (*Not looking straight at him.*) Are you . . . ?

DANNY. Everything's going exceptionally well, the family and (*Breezy smile.*) I'm making a surprising amount of money now, and got a new car, not a Porsche or a BMW you'll be pleased to hear, in fact I should be able to just about pay the expense of this trial if you lose. (*Sharp smile.*) That was a joke, heavily disguised probably, but it was one. I have some interesting clients at the moment. (*Serving himself food.*) I'm doing the books for Marwood and Price Ltd, you know the advertising agency, quite a newsworthy outfit at the moment, as well as Marwood (*Determinedly.*) we have Levant and Dorking, Parks and Greenwell, Petrie Associates, Kirsten and Bywater . . . the Gresham Company, T. Wyngate, that's another big one, Barbray and . . .

BILL (*very sharp*). Right Danny. (*Looking up at them.*) Why're you two here now?

ROXANNA. To see you.

DANNY. Yes, we felt we had some unfinished business.

BILL (*sharp*). What business?

DANNY. I mean we felt we were losing touch with one another – needed to straighten that out.

BILL. OK now, what do you really want?

ROXANNA. There's nothing else – isn't that enough.

BILL (*suspicious*). Is it?

ROXANNA (*warm*). Come on, let's eat, have you tried this wonderfully leathery meat, the gravy is like mud, repulsive over-cooked English food, it's perfect for this place – it's like eating the furniture.

BILL. You don't think I should be taking this libel action do you?

ROXANNA. Did I say anything?

BILL. I'm asking you and I want it straight Roxanna, as usual.

Momentary pause, ROXANNA *responding like she used to be with him.*

ROXANNA. OK then, you shouldn't. You should have floated above the gossip, especially as they were prepared to settle – amazingly. (*Looking straight at him.*) But you really wanted to have another go in public again anyway, didn't you? Because the results of your work are taking much longer than you expected, and you want applause for what you're doing. (*Warm smile.*) You shouldn't, but you do.

BILL (*watching her*). Do I?

ROXANNA (*lightly*). Why worry about anybody thinking you're failing – I couldn't care a fuck about that.

BILL. Go on.

ROXANNA (*animated*). In fact it's quite funny watching people block their ears in court, as you start spouting from the witness box, they practically duck down in their seats. (*Very warm.*) Often I think you sort of leave a trail of people doing that, wherever you go. (*She smiles.*) Are you going to erupt now, turn the table over? (*Slight pause.*) You are going to win the trial anyway, I just meant it makes your detractors extremely happy hearing those things said about you in court, but it's no big deal, this meeting is infinitely more important. (*Looking at him.*) How did I do? (*Lightly.*) Don't shrink back like that Dad, what's the matter?

Pause.

BILL. Please don't smoke in here.

ROXANNA. What?

BILL. I don't want to breathe your smoke.

ROXANNA. OK, I won't come near you – I'll sit over here. There'll be an exclusion zone right round you.

BILL. I'm asking you, please put that cigarette out at once.

ROXANNA (*startled*). OK . . . (*Moving away.*) Jesus, this is like having lunch with Henry the Eighth – (*Nervous.*) Just relax, OK.

Momentary pause.

DANNY. No, no, Dad she's wrong. I think you had to fight this action, you were absolutely right.

BILL (*quiet*). I'm glad somebody thinks so.

DANNY. Without doubt. And you're doing marvellously.

BILL. Yes, Danny, you told me. (*Slight pause, looking up.*) There's something else, isn't there?

DANNY. If I have one small criticism . . . (*Stops.*) No . . .

BILL (*calmly, not looking up*). Go on.

DANNY. It is – don't take this wrong – I think it's a mistake to keep on saying any idiot can make a fortune.

BILL. I didn't say that.

DANNY. Ridiculing financial security.

BILL. I have never done that.

DANNY. It's the most important aspiration for a great number of people, surely it drives everything . . .

BILL (*cutting him off*). Danny you don't have to tell *me* these things, (*Quieter.*) you really don't.

DANNY. I think you under-estimate how it looks coming from you, saying there's nothing to it, a million's a million, anybody can do it before breakfast, it can appear arrogant.

BILL (*dismissive*). You have misunderstood what I meant Danny. You can't have been listening. (*Quiet, withdrawn.*) But I hear what you say, I have noted it (*Sharp.*) OK . . .

ROXANNA. Why don't you ring a bell every time you want the subject changed. (*Lightly.*) He has a point after all. Come on you're not eating – the mushy sprouts are getting cold.

Pause.

DANNY (*staring straight at him*). But overall I think you've been really very clever.

BILL (*looks up*). Clever . . . in what way?

DANNY. In how you've managed things. Of course you believe in your building project, I realise, but some of the other things, most of the innovation schemes are deliberate tax losses, must be, and yet you have got all this publicity and kudos, in some quarters anyway, out of these schemes. It's brilliant, out of ideas that are going to be losers deliberately, like the extraordinary road-rail project.

BILL (*quiet*). So that's why you're here, you've come to provoke me, Danny.

DANNY (*determinedly, facing up to him*). Of course not, I'm just trying to make sense of your financial operation.

ROXANNA. Danny, maybe this isn't the time to try to have things out.

DANNY. I've been thinking about it so much lately and I believe I understand it now.

BILL (*quiet*). I don't think you probably have ever really understood Danny. (*His arm shoots out, catches* ROXANNA *by the wrist.*) While she . . . she on the other hand understands everything I'm trying to do, even more than she did before, but she pretends she does not, which is far far worse, (*Quiet, intense.*) and I expect what she's doing now, whatever it is, is not enough . . . is it Roxanna?

ROXANNA. Listen . . . (*Moving with plates.*) We're meant to be having a reunion. It's really hot, we're caged up in here – but we're going to make it work.

DANNY (*facing* BILL, *determined tone*). I did not understand I admit, how having made brilliant acquisitions earlier in your career being so far ahead of the field . . .

BILL. A little in front.

DANNY. No miles in front. I mean you had the chance, a real chance, of building a great consumer empire out of the cameras and gramophones . . . that sort of product – and now it could look like having made all your money out of these things you then promptly turned around and started attacking everyone for buying them. For possessing them. Couldn't it? I mean when you moved on to these visionary ideas – so long-term they don't even exist yet – I can't tell you how relieved people were, the people that had been the target of your criticism. They were jubilant, when you hit this visionary phase.

ROXANNA. Danny . . .

DANNY. But now I have a theory which explains all of this I think – which I'm trying to put . . .

BILL (*suddenly*). Danny – nothing you can say to me on this subject is of any interest whatsoever.

ROXANNA. This is lunch break in the High Court, we'll have lawyers running in here offering their services if we fight and I'm not paying! So please –

DANNY (*to* BILL). You can't say it's of no interest because you haven't heard it all.

BILL. Of course I can say that, because every time I look at you Danny, I see what I'm up against – you're a permanent reminder. Far too close to home.

DANNY (*sharp*). What do you mean by that?

BILL. I mean by that the sort of ignorance and pettiness, and lack of foresight, that is holding up a lot of my schemes.

ROXANNA (*loud.*) Don't talk like that – It's unforgiveable.

DANNY. It's OK Roxanna, I don't need your help, I can handle it.

BILL. It's true – you lack all curiosity about the ideas I'm backing, any sense of wonder, and you are quite, quite incapable of seeing their importance. Just like the people I have to deal with all the time.

DANNY (*strong*). That is not true and you know it.

BILL. Oh no? You think I should give up my projects, don't you. Go back into gramophones, into video recorders and all that shit. I CANNOT GO BACK. I WON'T GO BACK. And nothing I can ever do will make you see that – I've known that for a very long time now Danny.

DANNY (*sharp, facing up to him*). Really? I don't believe they're all without value anyway, your schemes, I think . . .

BILL (*savage smile*). You think one of them might show a glimmer of promise, do you Danny.

ROXANNA. This is my idea of hell, having this scene now, let's get out of here for fuck's sake, it's summer out there, break this up –

DANNY. You haven't allowed me to put my case, so you can't know what I feel about all your ideas. (*Straight at him.*) But I'll put it better at the end of today when –

BILL. There will definitely be no need for us to see each other at the end of today or indeed . . .

ROXANNA (*very strong to* BILL). That is enough – You *understand*.

BILL (*catching her by the arm*). As for you, I expect you put him up to this – this was all planned, my two children, conspiring to . . .

ROXANNA. You really think we'd do that – I think this is what *you* wanted to happen for some reason, so you needn't be bothered with us any more.

DANNY. What *I* was trying to do, if you'll let me finish for once in my life, I was trying to demonstrate something to you, that I'd made sense of your current situation, it came out wrong, but that doesn't mean –

BILL. No it didn't – it came out exactly as you meant it.

DANNY. Oh really, and how do you know that?

BILL. Because that's just the way you are Danny.

DANNY. Oh I forgot, you know everything about me of course even before I've thought of it! You're always right, whether it's the fucking road-rail vehicle or me, every time totally right. You say I don't listen, but you have never listened to anything I've said ever, never taken it seriously for a single moment . . . you made up your mind about me so early didn't you, I think you often couldn't even stand being in the same room with me (*Loud.*) could you?

BILL (*quiet, startled*). Danny . . .

DANNY (*near tears*). And I'm *not* going to let you make me cry either, you have never managed to make me – not going to let you now.

ROXANNA (*moving over*). That's right – why should we care what he thinks? Why should we worry for one moment? He just shrugged off his children when we didn't agree with him. (*Flicks the air.*) Surplus to requirements.

BILL. Roxanna – you know that's not true, that's not the case.

ROXANNA. We can do exactly the same, he never keeps in touch, he never tries to see us, scared to face his own children because they might tell him something he didn't want to hear – he couldn't care whether we exist or not. (*She moves.*) In fact it's really totally irrelevant what he says or thinks now.

BILL (*looking straight at her*). That's right Roxanna.

Pause. BILL sits in the middle of room eating a mouthful of his food. ROXANNA, watching him.

ROXANNA (*leaning by exit*). And unless I'm much mistaken, isn't there somewhere in this absurd building the audience you really want to be with, the court, waiting with baited breath for you, wondering where the hell you are?

BILL (*head spinning round*). Jesus, what's the time Roxanna?

Blackout.

Sound of passages, hum of hushed conversation mixed with footsteps hurtling down a long corridor.

Scene Five

The JUDGE staring down, round blubbery face, expressionless.
   QC stands waiting on the edge of the light staring into wings. Momentary pause. He glances up at the JUDGE.
   BILL arrives hurriedly by witness box, looks up at JUDGE, takes his place.

JUDGE. You are late. You are late back, Mr Galpin.

BILL. Am I? I was unavoidably detained . . . I apologise . . . my lord.

JUDGE. You have obviously found a class of catering in this building that I was unaware of. The whole process begins to disintegrate when lunch becomes more important than what goes on here – you will apologise to the court again.

BILL (*startled*). Again? Really? If that is considered necessary, I apologise to the court again. (BILL *glancing around*.)

JUDGE. Are you all right Mr Galpin?

BILL (*suddenly*). I'm quite all right.

JUDGE. Proceed.

QC. I want now Mr Galpin to move to one of the central issues of this case.

BILL (*cutting him off*). Good, about time, I had begun to think you weren't too keen to get there.

BILL's *manner abstracted, then suddenly focusing on* QC *then away.*

QC. It is true is it not that your large-scale building projects, the so-called road-rail network spreading over a piece of Africa *and* the controversial housing complex and 'invention park' in London have suffered massive delays?

BILL. Yes, yes, we know this. (*Sharp, correcting himself.*) But they are now back on schedule, very much so . . .

QC. That money, even your money couldn't make everything happen. That you were dependent on other factors, like the agreement of foreign governments and planning permission from local councils.

BILL (*not looking at him*). Yes, yes . . .

QC. And that you would very much like to quicken the process.

BILL, *a sharp mumble.*

I'm sorry. What did you say? I didn't hear that.

BILL. I said, you are stating the obvious.

BILL *gives the dangling microphone a shove – so it swings across like a pendulum.*

JUDGE. Mr Galpin, please try to keep still, and not disrupt the furniture.

QC. And in your attempt to speed up the process and clear the site in London of all the remaining tenants, we come to the moment when you hired Mr Hertie and Mr Clearsil.

BILL (*matter-of-fact*). Yes.

QC. Both of whom by an extraordinary coincidence are in Europe at the moment?

BILL (*hardly listening to him*). Means nothing, I asked them to come back myself.

QC. Now before we come to the strange sequence of events that followed, the fire in one of the shops, the breaking of windows,

BILL. That was kids.

QC. the late night phone calls, the spiral of alleged Rachmanesque behaviour . . .

BILL (*abstracted manner*). The alleged Rachmanism has already been examined by the police, at my request, and found to be groundless.

QC. I want to look at why you chose to delegate for the first time these –

JUDGE. Just one moment, for the benefit of the jury, I'm sure they know, but one or two of them are quite young, an explanation of the term Rachmanism is required.

QC. Of course my lord, Rachman was a slum landlord in the fifties and early sixties who employed men who used violence on his behalf to evict sitting tenants.

BILL (*suddenly focusing, provocative*). No, initially he was looked upon as a hero figure by the immigrant community, because housing conditions for them were so scandalously bad, he was one of the very few who would provide them with some . . . (*Stops.*) and it was only later –

QC (*sharp*). Yes, that's a very interesting interpretation Mr Galpin – why did you say that?

BILL. Because it's true.

QC. Is he a figure then with whom you identify?

BILL. That is not a serious question I hope, I was merely correcting a received opinion.

QC. And that is something you feel compelled to do in all your work is it? Provoking people out of complacency, correcting them when you feel they're wrong!

BILL (*beginning to lose patience*). I don't think I'm compelled – if I know about something, I say it. I've been looking into housing recently, so I naturally know about this.

QC. And just staying with this for a moment, would it be fair to say that you would like your name, obviously in a totally different way to Mr Rachman, but you would like it to be an ism?

BILL *mouths 'What' in astonishment.*

Become automatically associated in the public mind with something – in your case innovation?

BILL. Become an ism! (*Looking about.*) I can't answer such a dumb question.

QC (*sharp*). Put another way – you would like to be recognised as the ultimate patron of the age?

BILL (*flicking the microphone, letting it swing slightly*). Your questions are rapidly becoming complete gobbledegook. I've done what I've done partly because nobody else was doing it that much, OK? I don't know how on earth we got onto this.

QC. And just to complete the picture, you too, just like the figure we've been talking about, see yourself as a bit of an outsider . . . is that true?

BILL (*muttering out of the corner of his mouth, slight smile*). Can you believe this?

QC. In your case obviously an outsider in your own country – a person outside normal conventions?

BILL (*louder*). No I would have thought in almost every respect I'm a wholly conventional man. I've been married and divorced, I have voted Conservative nearly all my life, I have two troublesome children, one of whom is constantly telling me how conventional I am, despite my occasional exhibitionism in public. (*Looks around.*) I even watch a lot of television – an almost abnormally conventional picture.

QC. Yes – but you *also* see yourself as someone who has a lot to offer, isn't that the case? And someone who has not been listened to as much as he would like . . . ?

Silence. BILL *looks about, slight smile.*

JUDGE. Mr Galpin, will you please answer the question.

BILL (*dismissing the proceedings*). I'm not interested in that question. I don't think I can play any more I'm afraid.

JUDGE. What did you say, Mr Galpin?

BILL. I'm not going to play any more. Apart from everything else these questions have become absurd.

JUDGE. Your meaning is not clear Mr Galpin, are you dropping your action?

BILL (*glancing around*). No, I just don't want to continue for the moment . . . this interview is closed.

JUDGE. Mr Galpin you cannot just swat away the rest of your cross-examination, it makes a mockery –

BILL (*slight smile*). But I have to swat this round away. I must plead ill health or whatever you like, I don't care, it's extremely hot for a start (*Pointing at* JUDGE.) and you look as if you're shrinking in the heat (*Glancing about.*) and I don't see why you need worry, you're all getting paid enough! Right now, I just want to get the hell out of here as fast as I can – and I intend to.

ROXANNA's VOICE (*calling out angrily*). What on earth do you think you're doing?

Blackout.

Scene Six

ROXANNA *in spot front stage, standing between two models of the road-rail vehicle. The small model we have seen before, and a much larger model, at least five feet high, and twelve feet long, with its strange conical nose facing us.*

　ROXANNA *is in dark colours holding a winter coat over her arm, smoking, music gradually building behind her, almost subliminal at the beginning.*

ROXANNA. November 6th – it's been weird watching it, ever since that gruesome meal, the trial spattering on for a few more sticky days, he refuses to quit, forces it to a verdict and loses.

She pushes the small model in front of her with her foot.

And people are naturally thrilled to see a rich man actually lose a libel case, who can blame them!

She moves forward with machine.

There are few more pleasurable sights in the whole world than a rich man suing and then falling resoundingly on his arse.

Moving forward, astride the small machine, ironic tone.

And there is even better to come – by coincidence or not, the Director of Public Prosecutions announces they are re-examining the evidence of suspected harassment on the site Dad bought. There is no real evidence. Dad, who had never delegated in his life, hired two morons to manage the site who then took the money and fucked off somewhere. He'd been too busy and had become careless, dumb even. (*With feeling.*) *That's all.* But the threat of prosecution is being stretched out, a lingering slur, far more effective than an actual trial.

ROXANNA *sends small model rolling into wings.*

For those who have always found Dad deeply suspect, insufferable in fact, the arrogant 'self appointed patron saint of innovation' – it's such comforting news. 'And he brought it all on himself'? It's wonderful!

ROXANNA *moving over to large machine.*

And pictures of the road-rail vehicle have started to reappear
of course, with its eccentric nose. (*She gives the nose a sharp
tap.*) The snouter, and the same jokes are bobbing up again.
(*Moving along the machine.*) My kids now play with the model
we've got – it fills up most of our tiny garden.

*She climbs on top of the large model, her voice intense for a
moment.*

They travel on it fast through imaginary rain forests and up
the sheer face of the Himalayas.

She sits astride large machine.

And Dad – is responding with a vengeance. To prove himself
right.

She switches on the headlight on the model.

Working furiously to get the machines on the road. Trying to
pull free. He won't shut up!

*Holding her arms high over machine, she rides it as riding a
bucking horse.*

He is wounded and becoming more dangerous apparently, and
therefore it would be quite interesting, even exciting to be able
to talk to him wouldn't it? But it's impossible for me to get to
see him.

She gets off machine, moving forward.

It's the most extreme it's been. He won't take my calls. And
in these hustling times it seems not to be the atmosphere in
which you just meet people you want to see by chance in the
street.

Putting on winter coat, music getting louder behind her.

(*Sharp.*) It's ridiculous isn't it, comic even, here I am still
hungry to see him, craving for that to happen (*Very sharp.*)
which doesn't please me . . . and to have to go through
moods, that change so violently, plunging about. (*Angry.*) But
he'll be able to turn it round of course. All of this. For
himself. And me? (*Loud.*) I can stop it too . . .

Music loud behind her.

But at this precise moment on this winter evening, I find I'm heading for a large dark concrete pub in South London, with sleazy music coming out of it, because I'm hoping to catch a glimpse of my father. One of the few chances I've got.

ROXANNA *turns as the large vehicle is taken off, the tawdry music loud round her.*

Red and blue lights playing on the back wall, shadows, a lot of the stage in darkness. In the pool of light near back wall, a single bare chair, and a large easel.

In a group downstage stand DANNY, FRANCES *and* MICK, *with* GANT *very slightly separate. All are looking inappropriately well-dressed among the smoke and coloured lights. They keep glancing towards the single bare chair.*

ROXANNA *moves towards them. The sound of disco music from the other side of the wall continues, mixed with drunken shouts and hand clapping.*

ROXANNA (*glancing around, startled*). You sure we're in the right room, is he really going to do it here?

FRANCES. This is where he chose, oh yes. (*Glancing at* ROXANNA.) You look so pale Roxanna. (*Touching her.*) You're wasting away like this – is anything the matter?

ROXANNA *moving, smoking.*

DANNY. It's so perverse him being here, this concrete hole, there are cracks in the ceiling even, (*Glancing up.*) might get hit by something. (*Running his hand along wall.*) And everywhere is coated in this layer of mashed up crisps and other junk.

Music behind wall rises and dips.

ROXANNA. Yes, not to mention the beer mats and old durex sticking to your feet. (*Staring into darkness.*) There're dark puddles over there, full of their own form of pond life.

MICK (*as the music pounds*). He likes all this. He's played the town hall, got that out of the way, now he enjoys doing the rougher venues too. But will he be able to drown out the sound of the stripper next door?

ROXANNA (*staring around*). And he's going to be watched just by us, is he, and kids with paint on their faces.

GANT (*sipping drink*). Isn't it strange, he won't see some of the people he used to know – but he comes to a place like this.

FRANCES (*looking at* GANT, *very sharply*). No, it isn't, he trying to get support from the community for one of his most important projects, his great housing plan. The public inquiry is starting any day now (*Closing in on* GANT.) and he's up against the full conservation lobby so it makes perfect sense for him to be doing this (*Loud.*) OK!

GANT *impassive*.

ROXANNA (*withdrawn*). What's so strange is all of us coming to watch.

MICK. We can't keep away from him, any chance and we take it! (*Sharp smile.*) This collection of odd creatures compulsively following him round at night. But he arrives in his limo at the door of the pub, does his gig, and slips away without anybody getting close to him.

ROXANNA (*quiet to herself*). I am *not* compulsively following him.

FRANCES. He won't see anybody – I spend my life lying to people.

ROXANNA (*looking up*). He'll see nobody at all?

FRANCES. It's like a disease – even with me whole days go by when he'll only speak through the intercom.

DANNY (*confident*). It's because of what's happened obviously.

FRANCES. I don't know – but I think people have enjoyed seeing it happen to him far more than some crooked city type being investigated.

ROXANNA (*quiet, withdrawn*). For me that is the single most striking thing.

DANNY (*authoritative*). Of course – they know where they are with straightforward monsters. They can't place Dad, he takes an odd delight in pouring his money away at the same time as lecturing people about forward-looking investment. (*He moves.*) People find these contradictions ridiculous.

ROXANNA. You mean you do, Danny – (*Quiet to herself.*) . . . he was right about you, really.

MICK. I think in a way, we've grown old, and he hasn't.

FRANCES (*sharp*). That's true of me. I age a year every week at the moment.

DANNY (*sharp*). Somebody described it as his 'maiming energy', he attacks without creating in its place.

Sound of glass breaking on the other side of the wall mixed with laughter and shouts.

ROXANNA (*turning towards the noise of glass being smashed.*) Jesus . . . what a place.

DANNY (*ignoring this, carrying on*). And those times have gone anyway, when he really stood out. I wished he still did! The world's crammed with far richer men now and he doesn't own newspapers, he doesn't own satellites, or TV stations. (*Slight smile.*) He wasn't even interested in going into compact discs, his natural territory. In the current climate he's without influence. But I'm not sure we know the whole story yet, there may be investments we haven't been told about, when he reveals these, people won't be able to say the things they –

GANT (*suddenly*). I don't think he minds what people say.

ROXANNA (*turning on him*). How on earth do you know that?

GANT. Your father is impervious, he doesn't care about it, he rises above it all, it's one of the things that's admirable about him.

ROXANNA. He didn't rise above it, that was his great mistake. You stupid man. He cared too much what all you fuckers thought. (*Bearing down on him in corner, threateningly.*) He needs to show some results now, doesn't he!

GANT. Yes he does. He really went out on a limb your father . . . but I expect this setback will only be temporary.

ROXANNA. Really! Is that so? And what are *you* doing here anyway?

GANT (*staring straight back at her*). It's a public meeting. It was
advertised. I came.

ROXANNA. Come to have a gloat have you! Still passionately
trying to make your mind up about one of his projects (*By
wall.*) No doubt these smashed crisps everywhere are yours!

GANT. Mine? What on earth are you talking about!

ROXANNA. An achievement of your new fast food project, ending
up smeared all over here!

She is in front of him. GANT *up against wall.*

GANT. Don't be absurd, it's something totally different (*Loud.*)
that project – not remotely the same.

GANT *flinches away, as if* ROXANNA *is going to do him some
injury.*

ROXANNA. Don't worry you're not worth it. (*Savage smile,
leaning close.*) Or maybe you are! (*Dangerous, close.*) You know
you remind me of one of those middle-aged women who go to
boxing matches and try to get as close to the blood as possible
while remaining totally safe, he horrifies you and he excites
you at the same time, doesn't he? That's why you keep trying
to see him, keep coming back for more. (*Savage smile.*) You
need it.

GANT. You are wrong. (*Breaking away from her.*) You have never
understood have you, my admiration for your father is
genuine.

DANNY. Because that costs you nothing.

GANT. On the contrary you are wrong again, it has cost me my
peace of mind. (*Moving into shadows.*) Quite substantially.
Truly. There are moments when I see very clearly what I
should be doing. (*Disappearing into total darkness.*) Oh yes!

He's gone.

MICK. That bastard will always survive!

Fluorescent lights flick off and on.

(*Agitated, looks at lights.*) Is this the two minute warning, for his entry? *I* get nervous when I'm near him, more than before in fact. Because I was one of his most perfect projects, his illustrations of finding brilliance that had leapt from nowhere – where of course he's always believed the most original ideas come from.

DANNY. His romanticism, yes. If it was ever true, it certainly isn't any more.

MICK (*smiles*). I had some good ideas – I really think I did, I was going to be his superstar innovator. And I betrayed it all by going off to do something utterly banal and lucrative.

ROXANNA (*very sharp.*) Of course – we've all done the wrong thing as far as he's concerned.

Something falls in the darkness, near DANNY, *like a light rain of plaster from a crumbling ceiling.*

DANNY (*loud.*) God, it nearly did hit me too!

ROXANNA *moving to* FRANCES *as music from the stripper on the other side of the wall getting louder.*

ROXANNA (*downstage, urgent to* FRANCES). Did you give him my message?

FRANCES. Yes, he just said tell her I'll reply . . . sometime.

ROXANNA. That's not good enough, not at all. You've got to get me in to see him.

FRANCES. It's impossible – he even resents me still staying with him. And the more his isolation grows, the more I turn into the bustling automaton secretary I wanted never to become.

ROXANNA. It's unforgiveable of him – he always swore he'd never indulge in this sort of Howard Hughes remoteness and now look at him.

FRANCES. And you Roxy, look at you, it's most unlike you to pine after anything.

ROXANNA (*furious*). Pining! I'm certainly not doing that for him. I assure you. (*Then urgent.*) Frankie you will do this for me though, won't you, I just need this, terribly badly, to be able –

BILL *enters from the side, carrying a large folder.* ROXANNA *startled, as he brushes past.*

(*Instinctively.*) Dad? (*As he moves.*) Dad!

BILL *gives them just an abrupt nod as he passes, he's dressed in a pale jacket, jeans and his distinctive shoes, moving upstage.*

MICK (*nervous smile*). You know I think he looks more at home in this place than we do.

ROXANNA. I expect you're right, he likes it here . . . for some strange reason.

BILL *standing upstage in spot, his manner direct and unapologetic, effortless, his best performance.*

BILL. I'd like to welcome you all here (*Sharp smile.*) to this dark cracked hole in the ground. It has a compelling odour all of its own doesn't it! And it was a new and shining structure so very recently.

Music pounding behind him.

To warm you up, before I show you the building scheme, as a curtain raiser I want to show you these pictures, an artist's impression of the road-rail vehicle in action.

Showing large picture on easel of the machine drawn in motion.

A great engineering achievement as you can see, and close, so very close, to being a reality.

Moving, getting next picture ready.

MICK. He makes me ashamed with his unflinching belief in my ideas. He never gives up, does he, he's got more of a creator's commitment than I have.

ROXANNA. He's doing it on purpose, bringing those with him.

MICK (*loud*). It doesn't alter the fact, does it.

BILL. And you will be able to see these machines right here, in this very city. (*He smiles.*) Oh yes. In the Invention Park that will be going up in your midst, (*Inviting.*) where you will be able actually to walk in among the inventions, (*He smiles.*) nothing between you and them, feel them, touch them if you want. Yes. Ideas that are not ephemeral. (*Pointedly.*) Definitely not ephemeral. And the park will be surrounded by these great buildings, using completely new materials.

Stripper's music really loud from next door. BILL *holding up silvery drawings, we can half see in the light.* BILL *smiles.*

I think they are probably reaching a climax next door, but maybe these are even more stimulating, I'll be handing round these beautiful pale drawings of the buildings for you all to see.

With power, across the depth of the stage, in the dark, smoky atmosphere, with the music behind him.

We're facing a very important public inquiry, people say these buildings are strange shapes, alien shapes compared to the hideous clutter around them, not safe, nostalgic shapes, nor are they pastiche post-modernist buildings, expressing nothing about ourselves. NOR WILL THEY FALL TO PIECES.

Sharp smile, music really loud.

They will be like nothing you have ever seen before.

Blackout.

Scene Seven

The music from the concrete pub continues, fading gradually away, as ROXANNA *and* DANNY *stand together front stage, watching the back wall slide back.*
  The first thing we see is a great quantity of brown paper parcels, over two hundred spilled together, covered in different labels and stamps from all over the world. And then the large pile of unpacked belongings that dominated Act One, looking roughly the same as it did before, the suitcases packed up, the chairs, the carpets, except it now has many more old gramophones on it. It, too, has brown paper parcels littered over it.
  DANNY *and* ROXANNA *stand together, facing upstage, staring at the pile.*

ROXANNA. Jesus! (*Looking at* DANNY.) Did you know about all this? (*Moving towards the pile.*) These are the old gramophones he used to make – what's he doing with them?

DANNY. I don't know. I had no idea he'd kept all this stuff still. (*Swinging his arms.*) It's so cold in here.

ROXANNA. Yes – it almost looks like he's trying to barricade himself in, high up in this terrible concrete slab (*Moving around.*) covered in scaffolding out there, damp on the walls here. (*Looks at* DANNY.) I don't know how he ended up living in such a place.

DANNY. It's weird isn't it . . .

Both of them moving along the base of the pile of belongings, picking things up.

DANNY. Some of my things are still here Roxy – from way back! A few of yours too. (*Pushing among parcels, curious.*) I'd heard about these, the brown paper parcels sent to him by crank inventors from all over.

Shakes one parcel, it makes peculiar rattling noise.

DANNY. Full of so called ideas. He's been bombarded by them. It looks like he doesn't want to open them.

ROXANNA. How's his financial position now?

DANNY (*briskly*). On the face of it, he's lost nine-tenths of his money, maybe more. He's been spectacularly extravagant on his projects just recently, trying to hurry them, complete them, selling his assets, going for broke. And of course since the trial and everything that's followed . . . he's finding it impossible to raise more money. That's totally out. (*Sharp.*) Remember this is on the face of it. (*Looks at her, touches her arm.*) You know Frankie's right, you don't look well.

ROXANNA. I'm OK, just about, I'm beginning to feel older that's all.

DANNY (*gently, near her*). Cultivating the gaunt and pale look? (*Shrewd smile.*) You've got to forget about him you know Roxy. (*Breezy.*) You see I'm fine now. Absolutely. (*He turns.*) I overheard something about you and him the other day . . .

ROXANNA (*startled*). About me and him?

DANNY. Yes – this guy was saying you could tell Dad was mad
because unlike the normal run-of-the-mill millionaire who
wants to turn his mistress into say a film star – Dad wanted to
turn his *daughter* into an *engineer*!

ROXANNA (*icy*). Really?

DANNY (*gently*). Just lately I've been thinking about you and him
a lot, wondering again if there was ever, long ago of course,
this is difficult to put, but . . . (*Tentative.*) something going on
between you?

ROXANNA. Going on? You mean sex Danny, something sexual
between us. (*Loud.*) That what you mean? No, it was much
more interesting than that – we had that relationship because
I've felt his equal since the age of five. (*Quiet.*) Always knew
it . . .

FRANCES *enters*.

ROXANNA. Well?

FRANCES. I've told him you're here . . . he may come out, I
don't know.

ROXANNA. You've got to make him. If he doesn't – I'm never
going to try again. You can tell him that.

FRANCES. That won't work, his moods are terrible at the
moment, since he lost the public inquiry. (*With feeling, to
herself.*) The scheme was far too unconventional for them of
course. (*Instinctively tidying.*) I've given him the date when
I'm leaving, he hardly seemed to notice at all.

DANNY. After all these years he didn't say anything? (*To
ROXANNA.*) Look what's happened to Frankie – staying
here –

FRANCES. He's always treated me well – though sometimes I had
to ask him for a rise, and I've treated him well. But he wants
me to go now, definitely. I remind him of the past. I like to
think I've understood what he's trying to do, especially
recently. This'll sound stupid, ridiculous even, but we had a
kind of silent understanding, we did. I often knew what he

was thinking. But now it's too late, I can't talk to him, shut up here, I can do nothing with him . . .

BILL *has entered.*

BILL. That's right. (*Moving past* FRANCES, *he touches her arm, matter-of-fact.*) That's exactly right.

BILL, *appearance different. He's altogether more hesitant, suspicious, clenched. He sits upstage, a distance from them on a large chair at base of pile.*

You wanted to see me?

DANNY. Yes.

ROXANNA (*looking over at* BILL). What's this? What you doing right over there, that's ridiculous.

BILL. What do you want?

DANNY. I just wanted to wish you Happy Birthday. (*He stops.*)

ROXANNA (*circling*). Yes, Happy Birthday. (*Matter-of-fact glancing up.*) I like the celebratory shoes.

BILL (*quiet, distant*). Thank you.

DANNY. There. I . . .

Pause. DANNY *suddenly awkward, nervous smile.*

Lucky I didn't bring a gramophone as a birthday present isn't it.

BILL (*very quiet*). Yes Danny.

DANNY. I want you to listen . . . I just want to say everything will come right. I know you've made very clear you think I'm not capable of understanding, I know you won't believe this, but I do admire a lot of what you're doing, and I know, (*Loud.*) and don't dismiss this, you're going to produce a surprise turnaround, a sucker punch – some investment we don't know about. Yes. And it's not all dark out there, there've been a few sympathetic articles about what you've been trying to accomplish.

Pause.

BILL (*very quiet*). Do you do this as some kind of revenge Danny?

DANNY. You see you've deliberately misunderstood what I'm trying to say, (*Loud.*) you do this to me again and again (*Really angry.*) don't you?

BILL. I'd be obliged if you'd leave. (*Icy, to* FRANCES.) Could you take him out of here please – right now.

DANNY. Don't worry I'm going, I'm getting away from here. (*Furious.*) I don't need this I can tell you! Any of it! (*Loud, with authority.*) And I won't be back . . .

ROXANNA. Danny!

FRANCES (*running after him*). I'll have to go with you otherwise you won't get out of here, all the security systems and locks he's had put in, (*With feeling at exit.*) it's typical of what's been happening.

ROXANNA. Frankie, get him back now, Danny! . . . (*Turning, loud.*) He's only trying to show you he exists for chrissake, because you've always made it so clear what you think of him – haven't you?

BILL *sits upstage, very still.*

BILL. And what do you want Roxanna? (*Sharp, flicking his fingers.*) Come on.

ROXANNA. So you're putting the clock on me already – 'granted' a few minutes in your presence and then out. (*Loud, moving.*) What's going on here anyway? These heaps of old gramophones, it's ghoulish – why've you shut yourself up like this, in this slab of a building, of all places?

BILL (*quiet, dangerous*). Roxanna – I want to know what you've come for?

ROXANNA. Stop doing that – I worked out what I was going to say, but it's gone now, (*Loud.*) completely vanished, this is not what I planned . . . (*Moving backwards and forwards.*) You see what happens – (*Really angry.*) and stop trying to make me so nervous, OK! Just stop it.

BILL (*quiet*). I know why you are here Roxanna, it's simple, you are going to tell me, you haven't decided how, but in a moment you will start telling me I haven't done what I intended to do (*Derisive.*) in your opinion, that I haven't begun to achieve what I set out to, you can't wait to list –

ROXANNA (*startled*). You think I came to do that? (*Sharp, dismissive.*) I don't care about any of the –

BILL (*suddenly lashing out*). Precisely. You don't care at all do you. That's absolutely clear.

ROXANNA. I didn't mean that, you know I didn't. (*Really nervous.*) Jesus, is this what it's going to be like trying to say anything to you now? If I say the wrong thing, I get attacked? (*She moves.*) I don't think you've failed, you clearly do, retreating up here, into this isolation ward. (*Looking at him.*) Are you going to scream at me now, go on, that should be worth one. Shouldn't it?

Turning to model of road-rail vehicle on pile.

You haven't done all you wanted obviously – sometimes you came very close, closer than I ever thought. (*Quiet, with model.*) For what it's worth now, I like some of the projects, the ones that disorientated people, this for instance with its nose, its fantastically perverse snout, like something out of a children's book, it's a wonderful idea this machine.

BILL (*very sharp, watching her*). Is it? You didn't always think like that Roxanna – and I'm not at all sure you do now.

ROXANNA. On to that now are you? Going to start throwing things back at me? You haven't forgiven me I know and I have *certainly* not forgiven you. (*Turns.*) Jesus you've hurt me.

BILL (*cold*). That's interesting. I've hurt you. What on earth do you mean? You turned away from everything you were good at, the work you should have done, from all the things –

ROXANNA (*loud*). I had to do that, of course. I had to get away from you.

BILL (*contemptuous*). That's rubbish – that's far too easy, and also totally untrue.

ROXANNA. How do you know? I don't want to go into this anyway. (*Turns suddenly.*) OK, I didn't want to be interested in those things but I was, despite myself, drawn towards . . .

BILL (*jabbing finger*). You were that's the point.

ROXANNA (*loud*). I didn't want to be!

BILL. Because for some unknown reason you were scared of it, that's what's unforgiveable.

ROXANNA. No. No, it was too much work or . . . I don't know, what does it matter now for chrissake. (*She moves.*) I probably wasn't any good really, you wanted to create a prototype out of me, set an example with your own daughter for the rest of the world to see, didn't you, at the very least create an apprentice for your work. You weren't right about me at all.

BILL. That's rubbish again. You could have done a lot more than me if you'd let yourself, maybe a great deal more, I was right without a doubt.

ROXANNA. Of course! Of course you were! You always are, I forgot, how stupid of me. (*Loud, provocative.*) We'll never know thank God anyway – will we!

She moves, strong.

Suddenly it all makes sense why you're here doesn't it, locking yourself up in decaying concrete buildings. It's to prove yourself *right* isn't it? You said this would happen, so you're inhabiting your own vision. (*Contemptuous.*) Naturally! Dwarfing yourself with all this junk.

BILL (*very quiet*). I don't advise you to go on with this Roxanna.

ROXANNA. Really – is that a threat? (*Moving.*) Trying to get rid of me like Danny . . .? I made a terrible mess of the break with you I know, I still dream about it sometimes. Trying to get away from you, I ended up thinking about you even more – that's what I didn't foresee. And it hasn't nearly healed, nearly stopped, but you know nothing about what's happened over the last few years, the moments of terror I went through because of what I thought I'd done to myself, the emptiness, till recently.

BILL (*quiet, straight at her*). I believe I told you what would happen if –

ROXANNA (*loud, mocking*). I thought you'd be able to resist

saying that, I really did, but no! Every time! (*Combative.*)
Come on – why don't you try some more . . . (*Suddenly
angry.*) You've made some mistakes as well, haven't you.
Plenty! – You got too impatient and careless didn't you,
because the work moved so slowly and you suddenly wanted to
make it all happen, show everyone, couldn't wait any longer
for the results, the ideas to be ready. (*With great force.*) Your
nerve should have held (*Loud.*) shouldn't it? I TOLD YOU,
DIDN'T I!

BILL (*sharp*). You see. You're doing it. You've started. Almost
exactly on time.

ROXANNA. Is that right . . . you sound so pleased. (*Moving,
upset.*) OK, I'm fucking all this up, being here . . . (*Quiet.*)
What do you want me to say, then?

BILL. I *knew* you'd come here to do this, you wonder now why I
kept away from you, because this is all you wanted, to come
and stare –

ROXANNA. That's not true.

BILL. To see me caged with all of this.

ROXANNA. You've caged yourself for a start.

BILL (*moving close to her, clenched*). Because this is all there is,
isn't there. As *you* know. (*Indicating gramophone.*) What should
have flowed from here, from these obsolete gramophones, from
all that junk, the ideas I should have made happen, they don't
exist. Not the important ones, nothing that really matters,
nothing that's finished. (*Close to her.*) I had the chance of
course, an opportunity like no other, but I can't make it
happen now. It's simple. It's gone.

ROXANNA. Yes.

BILL (*controlled, dangerous*). But of course that's no surprise to
you, because you always knew I was bound not to succeed,
didn't you?

ROXANNA (*quiet, watching him*). Yes.

BILL. But I don't believe that Roxanna, not at all. Not for one
moment.

He is very close to her, her head instinctively jerks back as if he is going to hit her.

What you doing that for? (*He looks at her, quiet, clenched.*) Why should I do that?

He moves her head, so she's facing him, holds it for a moment, his hands either side of her face.

ROXANNA. I don't know – because you want to. (*Staring straight back at him.*) Because I'm here now. (*She moves her head.*) Because you know you may not get another chance.

BILL. Probably not, no. (*Staring at her.*) I know that.

He holds her by one arm, very tight, he's hurting her, looking at her.

You're going to start telling me what people are saying about me, out there – just like Danny . . . The pleasure they're getting, from all of this. (*Holding her tight.*) Come on.

ROXANNA. You care about that!

BILL. Yes. (*Staring at her.*) Come on. (*Provocative.*) Start.

ROXANNA. Why should I want to do that? (*Slight pause.*) I came here . . . I couldn't stand what had happened between us any more. I won't put up with that any more, finding myself trailing after you, all over the city.

BILL (*moving off briskly*). I have things to do now, things to see to, Roxanna. So goodbye. If you find Frances, she should be able to show you a way of getting out of here.

ROXANNA (*furious*). Oh no, don't you walk away from this, don't you dare walk away from me now, just when I was telling you . . .

BILL *is moving away*, ROXANNA *pulls at him fiercely as he goes, holding on, restraining him.*

ROXANNA. Come back – don't you do this – come back here.

Forcibly, holding on to him, he turns, catches hold of her arm.

BILL (*with passion*). You should never have gone, you stupid, stupid girl – you wasted all that time, all those years.

ROXANNA *cries, angry tears, pushing her head at him.*

BILL. You don't realise how much you could have done.

ROXANNA (*angry, crying*). No, no . . . You're not right. You aren't. I'm not having you tell me this – it would never have happened . . . never . . . I'm sure . . . (*Pause.*) I am.

Pulling away, moving across.

Understand. *Understand that?*

BILL (*strong*). No. I don't.

Silence.

ROXANNA. That's what you mind most about, not making me do that . . . share your work.

BILL (*sharp*). Is it?

ROXANNA. I would have made absolutely no difference to all of this. (*Indicating models on pile.*) None. And you know it.

BILL (*watching her*). I thought you were just telling me how you would have changed everything, weren't you Roxanna, your fearless approach, how you would have made me . . .

ROXANNA. No difference. (*Louder.*) My advice from time to time would have changed nothing.

ROXANNA *moving towards him, formidable.*

BILL (*staring back at her*). Roxanna, we don't know that, do we?

ROXANNA (*by him, touching his face for a moment*). Even if I have always been older than you, don't you think? Since the age of five, or even three perhaps – and what good has it done me . . . what good at all. (*Looks at him.*) You frighten people you know, because you have this curious belief in oddly shaped machines, and buildings . . . and all the rest.

BILL. And I couldn't even make my own daughter see it – want to be part of it.

ROXANNA. Sometimes you did – isn't that enough?

BILL. No – *that is not enough.*

Slight pause.

ROXANNA. So what would be? (*She glances up.*) No, I didn't mean that, don't try, it's much much too late, I'm not coming to work for you – Jesus one is never safe with you is one! Come anywhere within range . . . ! We can't go back to that, you understand, it's impossible, I've forgotten everything I knew.

BILL. I could change that quite quickly.

ROXANNA. There's no chance. I'm not being pulled back. We can't.

Pause.

BILL (*flicking his fingers*). If, if I was to ask you . . .

ROXANNA. No. (*Moving off.*) NO!

BILL. – to stay a little longer tonight. Just . . .

ROXANNA *turns.*

ROXANNA. That's possible Dad. Of course. A little longer.

BILL (*sharp*). That's allowed is it.

ROXANNA. Tonight, yes. That's all. Do you understand?

Pause. Noise of creaking scaffolding.

Christ, that creaking, and the flapping plastic. You like that don't you? This place is really falling to bits, dissolving around us.

BILL. Its walls crack a little more each day. It's hardly lasted a handful of years.

ROXANNA. You're the only person I've ever met who finds quick decay comforting, that loves bits of loose masonry and wafer thin walls, you probably lean out of the window high up here and scrape another piece off yourself. (*Moving over to the pile.*) It's horribly cold though, the draught . . . and all these accumulated things here.

BILL (*moving towards pile*). Some of that is a reminder of better times. (*Straight at her.*) Isn't it?

ROXANNA. You should get rid of it all . . .

ROXANNA *begins to climb among the belongings and among the brown paper parcels.*

These are different of course – these parcels, you ought to open them, you can't just leave them, they're stranded up here at the moment.

BILL. They're all from lunatics.

ROXANNA. Probably, yes.

BILL. So it doesn't matter.

ROXANNA. Doesn't it?

BILL (*savage smile, animated, as he clambers among parcels*). It is deeply depressing opening one mad parcel after another I can tell you – this is exactly what my detractors would love to see Roxanna, me strutting about in an ocean of grubby paper parcels, becoming the king of the brown paper bags. Drowning in them. Some of them – look – even have strangely formed handwriting on them, huge childish handwriting, and they make weird sounds, or little bells start ringing when you turn them over with your foot. And in every one a crazy idea, a ludicrous notion about the future, a crank waiting for you, ready to leap out as soon as you raise the lid.

BILL *stands completely surrounded by brown paper parcels.*

This is not exactly what I had in mind.

ROXANNA. Fuck what anybody else thinks . . . we don't know what's here do we?

BILL. The only comforting thing is, they are really slowing down now, arriving in just a trickle.

ROXANNA. I don't think that's comforting, I think that's rather frightening. (*She's moving on pile.*) You're going to open some now, I think. I'll help until I have to go (*Firm.*) which is soon, very soon. (*Climbing on top of pile.*)

It probably is all junk . . . there're some really oddly shaped parcels here, but . . . Jesus, look at this! This one is eight years old, it's been sitting here for all that time. (*Lifting parcel.*) Here, catch, start on that one.

She stands on top of pile, BILL watching her.

ROXANNA (*warning*). Don't you look like that Dad . . . What you looking at?

BILL (*staring at her for a moment, slight pause*). Nothing, Roxanna.

ROXANNA. Good. Then get to work.

Sitting far apart on the great pile of brown paper parcels, they begin to open them.

Fade.